At Issue

| Teen Smoking

Other Books in the At Issue Series:

At Issue

|Teen Smoking

Roman Espejo, Book Editor

GREENHAVEN PRESS
A part of Gale, Cengage Learning

GALE
CENGAGE Learning·

Farmington Hills, Mich • San Francisco • New York • Waterville, Maine
Meriden, Conn • Mason, Ohio • Chicago

Elizabeth Des Chenes, *Director, Content Strategy*
Douglas Dentino, *Manager, New Product*

For more information, contact:
Greenhaven Press
27500 Drake Rd.
Farmington Hills, MI 48331-3535
Or you can visit our Internet site at gale.cengage.com

For product information and technology assistance, contact us at

Gale Customer Support, 1-800-877-4253
For permission to use material from this text or product, submit all requests online at www.cengage.com/permissions.

Further permissions questions can be e-mailed to permissionrequest@cengage.com.

Articles in Greenhaven Press anthologies are often edited for length to meet page requirements. In addition, original titles of these works are changed to clearly present the main thesis and to explicitly indicate the author's opinion. Every effort is made to ensure that Greenhaven Press accurately reflects the original intent of the authors. Every effort has been made to trace the owners of copyrighted material.

LIBRARY OF CONGRESS CATALOGING-IN-PUBLICATION DATA

Teen smoking / Roman Espejo, book editor.
   p. cm. -- (At issue)
  Includes bibliographical references and index.
  ISBN 978-0-7377-6866-4 (hardcover) -- ISBN 978-0-7377-6867-1 (pbk.)
  1. Teenagers--Tobacco use. 2. Smoking. 3. Tobacco use--Prevention. I. Espejo, Roman, 1977-
  HV5745.T445 2014
  362.29'60835--dc23
                                         2013043521

Printed in the United States of America
1 2 3 4 5 6 7 18 17 16 15 14

Contents

Introduction

Nicotine is just one of about four thousand chemicals in a burning cigarette, but it gets the most attention for its effects. After being absorbed in the lungs, nicotine hits the bloodstream, instantly causing the adrenal glands to release epinephrine. This hormone stimulates the nervous system, elevating the heart rate, blood pressure, and respiration. Within ten to twenty seconds, nicotine reaches the brain and increases its level of dopamine, a neurotransmitter that helps control the brain's reward and pleasure center as well as emotions. This mechanism is thought to play a key role in dependency and abuse. "For many tobacco users, long-term brain changes induced by continued nicotine exposure result in addiction—a condition of compulsive drug seeking and use, even in the face of negative consequences,"[1] states the National Institute on Drug Abuse (NIDA). Smokers, then, become trapped in the cycle of quitting and falling back into the habit. "When an addicted user tries to quit, he or she experiences withdrawal symptoms including irritability, attention difficulties, sleep disturbances, increased appetite, and powerful cravings for tobacco," continues NIDA.

Numerous experts claim that the still-developing adolescent brain is particularly vulnerable to the addictive properties of nicotine and, therefore, a major focus of tobacco research. In 2012, Mark Rubinstein, a researcher at the University of San Francisco, California's School of Medicine, led a study on how teen smokers metabolize the substance. Rubinstein and his team used the byproduct cotinine to measure the process, enabling the study to include youths who smoked lightly or not every day. "We looked at rates of nicotine metabolism in

---

1. National Institute on Drug Abuse, "DrugFacts: Cigarettes and Other Tobacco Products," December 2012. http://www.drugabuse.gov/publications/drugfacts/cigarettes-other-tobacco-products.

164 adolescent smokers and found that slower metabolism was associated with more self-reported addiction and more cigarettes smoked,"[2] he claims. "The brains of slower metabolizers are likely being exposed to greater amounts of nicotine for a longer period of time." The finding surprised Rubinstein, as it counters research on adults and nicotine metabolism. "This was really interesting because it is the opposite of what is found in most studies of adult smokers, in which faster metabolizers smoke more and are thought to be more addicted," he explains.

Another study, published in 2007, purports that teen smokers show signs of being hooked on nicotine faster than previously established. It is commonly believed that dependence occurs with smoking five cigarettes a day. Monitoring 1,246 sixth-grade students over a four-year period, researcher Joseph R. DiFranza and his team at the University of Massachusetts Medical School found that 10 percent of smoking adolescents became addicted within two days of their first cigarette and 25 percent experienced withdrawal symptoms with smoking a few cigarettes a month. "While smoking one cigarette will keep withdrawal symptoms away for less than an hour in long-time smokers, novice smokers find that one cigarette suppresses withdrawal for weeks at a time,"[3] DiFranza maintains. "One dose of nicotine affects brain function long after the nicotine is gone from the body. The important lesson here is that youth have all the same symptoms of nicotine addiction as adults do, even though they may be smoking only a few cigarettes per month," he contends.

Some research even proposes that nicotine can prime the adolescent brain for addiction long before a teen inhales his

2. Quoted in "Teens May Be More Susceptible to Nicotine Addiction," Clinical & Translational Science Institute, July 30, 2012. http://ctsi.ucsf.edu/news/about-ctsi/teens-may-be-more-susceptible-nicotine-addiction.
3. Quoted in "Inhaling from Just One Cigarette Can Lead to Nicotine Addiction: Kids Show Signs of Addiction Almost Immediately," *ScienceDaily*, July 6, 2007. http://www.sciencedaily.com/releases/2007/07/070703171843.htm.

or her first cigarette. A 2013 study by German researchers at Technische Universität Dresden indicates that mothers who smoke during pregnancy potentially alter the development of their babies' brains—the reward and pleasure center, in particular. In addiction simulations with youths between thirteen and fifteen years old, the researchers found that those exposed to nicotine in utero domonstrated less activity in this region of the brain, which is associated with persistently seeking a "high" and chemical dependency. "The weaker responsivity of . . . prenatally exposed adolescents may represent a risk factor for substance use and development of addiction later in life,"[4] they assert. "This result highlights the need for education and preventive measures to reduce smoking during pregnancy."

Nonetheless, nicotine as a highly addictive substance is under dispute. In a 2009 research presentation to NIDA, Peter Killeen, emeritus professor of psychology at Arizona State University, declared that nicotine addiction does not exist. "A large portion of the research on tobacco studies is done on nicotine. But the research has not been very reinforcing,"[5] Killeen argues. "Studies have shown that none of the nicotine replacement therapies—chewing gum, inhalers, patches—none of those are addictive." He proposes that the release of monoamine oxidase inhibitors (MAOIs) during smoking, which regulates dopamine, is the main culprit. "When you put together something that directly releases dopamine and another thing that helps the brain clean up excess dopamine, you've got a one-two punch," Killeen states. "It is my hypothesis that it's a combination of nicotine with some of these other chemicals that causes the powerful addiction."

---

4. Quoted in Alexandra Sifferlin, "Mothers Who Smoke While Pregnant Put Kids at Risk of Substance Abuse," *Time*, June 20, 2013. http://healthland.time.com/2013/06/20/mothers-who-smoke-while-pregnant-put-kids-at-risk-of-substance-abuse.
5. Quoted in Jessica Testa, "Professor: Nicotine Does Not Cause Cigarette Addiction," *The State Press* (Tempe, AZ), September 3, 2009. http://www.statepress.com/archive/node/7194.

The neurological effect of nicotine, especially on adolescents, will continue to be investigated, as nine out of ten smokers pick up the habit before turning eighteen years old. Furthermore, other factors—from the marketing tactics of tobacco companies to the rising popularity of electronic cigarettes—are flashpoints in the smoking debate. *At Issue: Teen Smoking* probes these and other related issues, presenting a diverse range of statistics, analyses, and views on underage tobacco use.

1

Teen Smoking Is Declining

Monitoring the Future

Funded by the National Institute on Drug Abuse, Monitoring the Future is a project of the University of Michigan's Institute for Social Research that surveys youth substance abuse each year.

A 2012 annual survey of teens in grades eight, ten, and twelve demonstrates that smoking among the age group continues to decline. According to researchers, the overall percentage of students that reported smoking in the prior thirty days had dropped from 11.7 percent to 10.6 percent, reflecting a 9 percent reduction in a single year. This may potentially prevent thousands of premature deaths and serious diseases attributed to smoking. Furthermore, the survey shows that the perceived availability of cigarettes among students has dropped and some attitudes and beliefs against smoking are at their highest levels recorded. Trends regarding other forms of nicotine use—from smokeless tobacco to hookahs—have either declined modestly or stabilized after increases in consumption in previous years.

The 2012 national survey results from the Monitoring the Future [MTF] study show a continuation of the declines in teen smoking in all three grades under study—grades 8, 10, and 12. Based on annual surveys of 45,000 to 50,000 students, the researchers found that the percentage saying that they smoked at all in the prior 30 days fell for the three grades combined, from 11.7% to 10.6%—a statistically significant drop.

Monitoring the Future, "Decline in Teen Smoking Continues into 2012," www .monitoringthefuture.org, December 19, 2012. Copyright © 2012 Monitoring the Future. All rights reserved. Reproduced with permission.

"A one percentage-point decline may not sound like a lot, but it represents about a 9% reduction in a single year in the number of teens currently smoking," observed Lloyd Johnston, the principal investigator of the study. "Such a reduction can translate eventually into thousands of premature deaths being prevented, as well as tens of thousands of serious diseases." More than 400,000 Americans per year are estimated to die prematurely as a result of their smoking cigarettes; and most smokers begin their habit in adolescence.

There was some evidence from the study that in 2010 the long-term decline in teen smoking might have come to a halt, but the decline resumed in 2011 and has continued into 2012 with statistically significant declines both years. An increase in the federal tax on tobacco products, instituted in 2009, may have contributed to this recent decline in smoking in this age group, according to the investigators.

The percentages of 2012 teens saying that they personally disapprove *of smoking are also at the highest levels seen in this study: 89%, 86%, and 84% for grades 8, 10, and 12 respectively.*

The Monitoring the Future study, which has been tracking teen smoking in the United States for the past 38 years, found that between 2011 and 2012 the percentage of students reporting any cigarette smoking in the prior 30 days (called 30-day prevalence) has decreased among 8th graders from 6.1% to 4.9% (a statistically significant decrease), among 10th graders from 11.8% to 10.8%, and among 12th graders from 18.7% to 17.1%. "While the improvement in the smoking numbers for just this one year is important, the longer term declines have been really striking," Johnston said. "Since teen smoking reached a peak around 1996–1997, the rates of current (past 30-day) smoking have fallen by about three fourths among 8th graders, two thirds among 10th graders, and half among 12th graders."

One reason that the current smoking rates have declined so sharply is that the proportion of students who *ever tried smoking* has fallen quite dramatically. In 1996, 49% of 8th graders had tried cigarettes, but by 2012 only 16% had done so, a two thirds drop in smoking initiation over the past 16 years. Further, the initiation of smoking is still falling significantly among 8th and 10th graders.

These estimates come from the study's national surveys of 45,000 to 50,000 students in about 400 secondary schools each year. The study was designed by and is directed by a team of research professors at the University of Michigan's Institute for Social Research, and since its inception has been funded through research grants from the National Institute on Drug Abuse—one of the National Institutes of Health.

Perceived Availability

Eighth- and 10th-grade students are asked how difficult they think it would be for them to get cigarettes, if they wanted them. This *perceived availability* has shown substantial declines since 1996. The 8th graders have shown the sharpest decline—from 77% saying they could get cigarettes "fairly easily" or "very easily" in 1996 compared to 51% in 2012. Perceived availability among 10th graders fell from 91% to 73% over the same interval. "Although there has been some real progress made in reducing the availability of cigarettes to those who are underage—particularly to the youngest teens—it is clear that the majority of teens still think they can get cigarettes fairly easily," Johnston said.

Attitudes and Beliefs About Smoking

Nearly two-thirds of 8th graders and about three-quarters of 10th and 12th graders in 2012 say they see a great risk of harm to the user from pack-a-day smoking. These figures have increased substantially since the mid-1990s, when *perceived risk* was at its recent lowest levels; the 2012 figures are the highest ever recorded for all three grade levels. The percentages of 2012 teens saying that they personally *disapprove* of smoking are also at the highest levels seen in this study: 89%, 86%, and 84% for grades 8, 10, and 12 respectively.

Other attitudes toward smoking and smokers have changed in important ways, as well, during much of the period of decline in cigarette use. These changes included increases in preferring to date nonsmokers (currently around 80% of teens say they do), strongly disliking being around people who are smoking, thinking that becoming a smoker reflects poor judgment, and believing that smoking is a dirty habit. All of these negative attitudes about smoking and smokers rose to high levels by 2007, but they have either leveled or begun to reverse since then.

Perceived risk, which MTF has shown to be an important determinant of trends for many forms of substance use, including cigarette use, also appears to have played an important role in the decline of smokeless tobacco use.

Johnston said, "Future progress in lowering teen smoking rates is likely to depend on there being further changes in the external environment—changes such as raising cigarette taxes, further limiting where smoking is permitted, bringing back broad-based anti-smoking ad campaigns, and making quit-smoking programs more available."

Smokeless Tobacco

The use of smokeless tobacco (which includes snuff, plug, dipping tobacco, chewing tobacco, and more recently "snus") also is assessed in the study. ("Snus" is singular, rhymes with "loose.") From the mid-1990s to the early 2000s, there was a substantial decline in smokeless tobacco use among teens— 30-day prevalence fell by one third to one half in all grades— but the declines ended and a rebound in use developed from the mid-2000s through 2010. Since 2010, however, there have been modest declines in all three grades. (The two-year declines are not statistically significant at any grade level, nor are the one-year or two-year declines for the three grades combined.) Thirty-day prevalence rates are now down by nearly two thirds (64%) from their peaks in the mid-1990s among 8th graders, and by over one third among 10th and 12th graders (39% and 35%). Thirty-day prevalence of smokeless tobacco use in 2012 is 2.8%, 6.4%, and 7.9%, among 8th, 10th, and 12th graders, respectively. The rates in each of the three grades are considerably higher for boys (4.0%, 11.2%, and 13.5%) than for girls (1.5%, 1.9%, and 1.6%). Use continues to be particularly concentrated in the South and Midwest and in non-urban areas.

Perceived risk, which MTF has shown to be an important determinant of trends for many forms of substance use, including cigarette use, also appears to have played an important role in the decline of smokeless tobacco use. In all three grades, perceived risk for smokeless tobacco rose fairly steadily from 1995 through 2004, as use was falling. However, there was not a great deal of fall-off in perceived risk subsequently, between 2004 and 2010, suggesting that other factors may have led to the increases in smokeless tobacco use in that time interval. These factors might include increased promotion of these products, a proliferation of types of smokeless tobacco products available, and increased restrictions on places where cigarette smoking is permitted. The leveling in smokeless use since 2010 may be attributable, at least in part, to the 2009 increase in federal taxes on tobacco. Perceived risk declined significantly in 2012 among both 8th and 10th graders, however, which could portend a future rise in use.

Hookahs and Small Cigars

Two of the latest developments to raise public health concern are the smoking of tobacco by using hookah (pronounced

"WHO-ka") water pipes, and the smoking of small cigars. The concern is that, as cigarette smoking continues to decline among adolescents, they will be enticed to smoke tobacco in these other forms, which still carry serious health risks. Questions about these forms of tobacco use in the prior 12 months (annual prevalence) were included in the survey of 12th graders for the first time in 2010, when 17.1% of 12th graders said that had used a *hookah* to smoke tobacco in the prior 12 months. This rate rose slightly to 18.5% in 2011 and then stabilized at 18.3% in 2012. Only 11% of 12th grade students in 2012 reported smoking with a hookah more than two times during the year, suggesting a considerable amount of light or experimental use. Males had only a slightly higher annual prevalence rate than females—20% versus 17%.

Smoking *small cigars* is about as prevalent a behavior as hookah smoking, with 12th graders having an annual prevalence of 20% in 2012. This is unchanged from 2011 and below the first reading on these products in 2010 (23.1%). Only 12% of the 12th grade students in 2012 indicated use on more than two occasions during the year. There is a larger gender difference for this form of tobacco use than for hookah smoking, with an annual prevalence of 27% among males compared to 13% among females. "We will continue to monitor these two forms of tobacco consumption to see if they represent a growing problem among youth, and we will be examining their use among young adults, as well," said Johnston.

Snus and Dissolvable Tobacco

In 2011 questions were introduced dealing with two more recent forms of tobacco use—snus and dissolvable tobacco. The question about *snus*—a moist form of snuff that is placed under the upper lip—asks on how many occasions in the past 12 month the student ". . .used snus (a small packet of tobacco that is put in the mouth)." Among 12th graders in 2011, 7.9% reported having used snus in the last 12 months; this rate remained unchanged in 2012. The proportion using more than two times was 5.2% in 2012. Clearly, snus made some inroads among 12th graders, but that seems not to be continuing. In 2012 the question about use of snus was added to the questionnaires given to 8th and 10th graders, and their annual prevalence rates are 2.4% and 6.9%. The pattern of use by subgroups of 12th grade students follows the pattern for all smokeless products generally, with use being much higher among males (14.1% versus 1.2% among females), noncollege-bound students (12.2% versus 6.6% among the college-bound), and those living in non-metropolitan areas (10.8% versus about 6.1% in large cities).

The question about *dissolvable tobacco* products asks on how many occasions in the past 12 months the student ". . . used dissolvable tobacco products (Ariva, Stonewall, Orbs)." These products, in the form of pellets, strips, or sticks actually dissolve in the mouth, unlike other forms of chewing tobacco. Among 12th graders in 2011 only 1.5% reported having used in the prior 12 months and in 2012 it was 1.6%. The question was introduced for the lower grades in 2012, and the annual prevalence rates there were 1.0% in grade 8 and 1.6% in grade 10. It appears that these products have not yet made significant inroads among secondary school students.

2

Teen Smoking Is Epidemic

US Department of Health and Human Services

The US Department of Health and Human Services (HHS) is the government's principal agency that provides essential human services and administers programs that address the health of all Americans.

Smoking is a global and national epidemic among youths and young people. While some advances have been made, almost one in four high school seniors is a smoker, and most continue to smoke in adulthood. Also, antismoking programs and widespread media stories on its serious dangers and consequences have failed to dissuade youths from using tobacco for generations. In fact, the data finds that smoking initiation rates among adolescents and young adults have remained the same for several years, occurring between the ages of fifteen and sixteen. As for decreases observed since the late 1990s in the rates and prevalence of tobacco use, declines have recently stalled, are often statistically insignificant, and vary among subgroups.

Tobacco use is a global epidemic among young people. As with adults, it poses a serious health threat to youth and young adults in the United States and has significant implications for this nation's public and economic health in the future. The impact of cigarette smoking and other tobacco use on chronic disease, which accounts for 75% of American spending on health care, is well-documented and undeniable. Although progress has been made since the first Surgeon

US Department of Health and Human Services, *Preventing Tobacco Use Among Youth and Young Adults: A Report of the Surgeon General*, 2012, pp. 3, 164–165.

General's report on smoking and health in 1964, nearly one in four high school seniors is a current smoker. Most young smokers become adult smokers. One-half of adult smokers die prematurely from tobacco-related diseases. Despite thousands of programs to reduce youth smoking and hundreds of thousands of media stories on the dangers of tobacco use, generation after generation continues to use these deadly products, and family after family continues to suffer the devastating consequences. Yet a robust science base exists on social, biological, and environmental factors that influence young people to use tobacco, the physiology of progression from experimentation to addiction, other health effects of tobacco use, the epidemiology of youth and young adult tobacco use, and evidence-based interventions that have proven effective at reducing both initiation and prevalence of tobacco use among young people. . . .

Nearly all tobacco use begins in childhood and adolescence. In all, 88% of adult smokers who smoke daily report that they started smoking by the age of 18 years. This is a time in life of great vulnerability to social influences, such as those offered through the marketing of tobacco products and the modeling of smoking by attractive role models, as in movies, which have especially strong effects on the young. This is also a time in life of heightened sensitivity to normative influences: as tobacco use is less tolerated in public areas and there are fewer social or regular users of tobacco, use decreases among youth. And so, as we adults quit, we help protect our children.

Young adults have the highest smoking prevalence among all age groups.

Cigarettes are the only legal consumer products in the world that cause one-half of their long-term users to die prematurely. As this epidemic continues to take its toll in the

United States, it is also increasing in low- and middle-income countries that are least able to afford the resulting health and economic consequences. It is past time to end this epidemic. To do so, primary prevention is required, for which our focus must be on youth and young adults. . . .

When Smoking Always Begins

Similar to the 1994 Surgeon General's report on smoking and health, this report finds that cigarette smoking virtually always begins in adolescence or young adulthood, as does the transition to daily smoking. In 2010, among adults aged 30–39 years, 81.5% of those who had ever tried a cigarette did so by the age of 18 years and 98.0% did so by the age of 26 years, based on NSDUH [National Survey on Drug Use and Health] data. Among those who had ever smoked cigarettes daily, the mean age of initiation was even younger; 88.2% first smoked by the age of 18 years and 99.0% first smoked by 26 years of age. Smoking initiation was most likely to occur in a young person's 15th or 16th year, which was also true in 1994. Adolescent and young adult initiation rates for cigarette smoking have been stable over the past 5 years. This finding is consistent with the idea that tobacco companies are successfully targeting young people in advertising and promotion efforts to attract new smokers.

Globally, the prevalence of tobacco use and the predominant products used among youth vary broadly.

Almost one-fifth of high school students are current cigarette smokers, and the prevalence rises with age; one-fourth of high school seniors are current cigarette smokers at present. Young adults have the highest smoking prevalence among all age groups. Males remain more likely than females to be current smokers in every age group except those aged 65 years and older. Similar to findings for adults, the prevalence of cigarette smoking among young people is highest for American Indians/Alaska Natives and Whites. The lowest prevalence of cigarette smoking among young people are among Asian and Blacks; in contrast, prevalence are lowest for Asians and Hispanics among adults. Since the late 1990s, smoking prevalence has decreased for both youth and young adults. Around 2003, however, the rate of decrease began to slow, such that any changes in the prevalence of current smoking from one iteration of a survey to the next were often statistically insignificant. These findings have led to concern that progress in decreasing youth smoking may have "stalled," or halted. Findings as to which youth demographic subgroups show a more or less pronounced stall are inconsistent across surveys. Overall, however, the most recent reports from both YRBS [Youth Risk Behavior Survey] and MTF [Monitoring the Future] suggest a stall in particular subgroups. In NYTS [National Youth Tobacco Survey], the prevalence of current cigarette smoking did not differ significantly between 2006 and 2009, the two most recent survey iterations. Only NSDUH has shown a continuing, statistically significant decline since 2002 in current smoking, although this decline may be limited to White youth since 2007.

Significant Differences in Use Patterns Are Masked

Smokeless tobacco is currently used by less than 10% of adolescents overall, but this finding masks significant differences in patterns of use among youth subgroups. The prevalence of current use among females is less than 2% except in a few Western states. Further, White male students are far more likely than males in other racial/ethnic subgroups to use smokeless tobacco, with the prevalence of current use among white male high school students at around 20%, based on YRBS data. Recent data from YRBS and MTF indicate that smokeless tobacco use may have increased among young White males in the latter half of the last decade. The prevalence of current use of cigars (including little cigars and cigarillos) is more than 10% for high school students but is more common among White male youth than among other youth subgroups. However, there are a few states in which female cigar use prevalence is around 5%, especially among Black females. The prevalence of cigar use among youth has been largely unchanged over the last few years with some evidence of an increase among Black females since 2007. Smokeless tobacco and cigars are often used by the same youth who smoke cigarettes. Indeed, more than one-half of White and Hispanic male high school students who use any tobacco product use more than one product, and just under one-half of Hispanic female high school students report the same. About 40% use both cigarettes and cigars; one-half of these youth use smokeless tobacco in addition. The prevalence of concurrent use of multiple tobacco products in the last 30 days among high school students has been stable for the past decade.

Global Use of Tobacco Varies Broadly

Globally, the prevalence of tobacco use and the predominant products used among youth vary broadly. Among the 140 countries and 11 territories, commonwealths, provinces, and regions that implemented the GYTS [Global Youth Tobacco Survey] between 2000 and 2007, cigarettes were the predominant form of tobacco used by 13- to 15-year-old students in the Americas, Europe, and Western Pacific regions. In the Eastern Mediterranean and South-East Asia regions, other forms of tobacco (such as smokeless tobacco, water pipes, or bidis) were more commonly used. The prevalence of current cigarette smoking among 13- to 15-year-old students varied by region, from 4.0% in Africa to 9.3% in the Americas; however, even within a region, broad variations in prevalence were noted. Although boys were more likely than girls to be tobacco users and current smokers in the majority of countries, the gender gap was narrow or nonexistent in some places; for example, the gap in current use of any tobacco product was statistically indistinguishable in Brazil (Rio de Janeiro), China (Shanghai), and the Russian Federation. In Spain and some South American [countries] (e.g., Argentina, Brazil, Chile, Uruguay), [even] cigarette smoking is more prevalent among girls than among boys.

3

Smokeless Tobacco Use Is Increasing Among Teens

Dustin Wyatt

Dustin Wyatt is a staff reporter for the Spartanburg Herald Journal *in South Carolina.*

Fewer teens smoke cigarettes, according to recent statistics. However, another form of tobacco is rising in use among the age group: smokeless tobacco, or "dip." Available in a variety of flavors and placed against the gums, it is easier for teens to conceal when they use it at school and more accessible to them than cigarettes at convenience stores. In addition, antitobacco programs have largely focused on smoking, and many youths are unaware of the dangers of dip, which actually places the user at greater risk of cancer because it directly contacts the mouth's lining. The use of dip tobacco among high school athletes is another trend that concerns some experts.

Fewer teens are smoking cigarettes these days, according to the Centers for Disease Control and Prevention.

That's the good news.

In Spartanburg, 73 percent of ninth- and 11th-grade youth surveyed thought it was "wrong for youth their age to smoke cigarettes," and 88.3 percent thought it was a "great risk" to smoke one or more packs per day, according to the 2010 youth survey conducted by the Spartanburg Alcohol and Drug Abuse Commission [SADAC].

But now, drug advocates are concerned about a different form of tobacco.

It comes in a circular can in a variety of flavors—wintergreen, mint, cherry, cinnamon. Users pack it against their gums and often spit it into a soda bottle.

"We are seeing a large trend among young white males who have moved from cigarettes to dip tobacco," said Mary Lynn Tollison with SADAC.

Relatively Easier Access

Youth seem to have a relatively easier time accessing the product, too, even though the legal purchase age for any tobacco is 18.

SADAC has sent underage youth into convenience stores to try to buy various drugs—such as cigarettes, alcohol, etc. If the merchant completes the transaction, they will promptly be ticketed.

Last year [in 2011], with a new grant from the United Way, these compliance checks in Spartanburg began focusing on smokeless tobacco. Tollison said the results weren't good.

She said 16.9 percent of underage teenagers walked out with newly purchased dip in their hands. The age group most commonly sold to? 15-year-olds.

With local ordinances pushing to get cigarettes off the streets and out of businesses, more people are turning to a more discreet, easier-to-hide form of tobacco. . . . Teens are using dip for the same reasons in school.

"Merchants have done a good job of putting cigarettes behind counters where youth must access them by going through a clerk," she said. "Some dip products continue to be at youth's reach on counters. Believe it or not, putting the products behind the counter prevents youth sales to some degree."

She said the commission's goal is for the percentage of sales to minors to drop below 10 percent.

With local ordinances pushing to get cigarettes off the streets and out of businesses, more people are turning to a more discreet, easier-to-hide form of tobacco, Tollison said. Teens are using dip for the same reasons in school.

"Many teens say it's easier to hide than cigarettes," she said.

Justin Fox, 17, doesn't use the drug, but he says he sees peers using dip in the classroom without teachers even noticing.

"They will have a Coke bottle out and spit in there, and the teacher never notices that the bottle is filling up rather than going down."

SADAC is encouraging schools to pay closer attention to dip use, asking resource officers and other officers to do their part and write more violations for possessing tobacco.

"Some schools and community centers follow their tobacco violations very strongly and refer students caught with tobacco to a four-hour Tobacco Education Class," Tollison said.

The class can be attended in lieu of paying the $101.88 tobacco possession fine.

Last year, of all of the students who went to the class for tobacco possession, 90 percent of them were caught with dip at school.

Educating Teens

Phillip Hudson, SADAC's senior prevention program coordinator, said 75 percent of smokeless tobacco users start as young as 14 years old. He says it's important that smokeless tobacco education start as early as middle school.

On a recent Saturday, Hudson discussed dip use with about 15 teenagers. The students, as part of SADAC's youth advisory board, will provide drug education and peer leadership in the community. This year, they will focus on smokeless tobacco for the first time in their 23-year history. To better serve the community and schools, they have to better understand the drug—and dip is something many teens don't know much about.

"We are all aware that cigarettes are addictive and cause lung cancer, and there's a lot of stuff out there saying 'Don't smoke cigarettes,'" Fox said. "But to tell you the truth, I don't really know a lot of the harmful effects that come from using dip. I mean, it makes your teeth yellow and it can be addicting, but there's not a lot of information about it."

Dr. Amy Curtis, a radiation oncologist with Spartanburg Regional Health Care System, said smokeless tobacco can be just as bad, if not worse, than cigarettes.

"One of the dangers of smokeless tobacco is that the chemicals that cause cancer are in direct contact with the lining of the mouth or the throat," she said.

She said she has heard of students keeping the tobacco pressed against their gums for an entire class.

"That is particularly dangerous because those chemicals are irritating the mouth for a relatively long period of time," Curtis said. "Smokeless-tobacco users can develop cancers decades earlier than cigarette smokers because the tobacco is right against the gum."

And the cancers, she says, are incredibly difficult to treat.

With a recent grant from the United Way, SADAC is focusing more attention on dip education and prevention than ever.

But Jeff Rogers, principal at Byrnes High School, says he hasn't noticed more teens using the drug.

"I think teenagers, especially in a rural area, have experimented with that for years, but we haven't noticed a surge recently."

He says the school has had awareness campaigns in the past that spoke to the dangers of smokeless tobacco.

Athletes Experimenting with Dip

During the recent Saturday meeting, students on the youth advisory board said they generally see a lot of athletes, such as baseball players, using the drug.

Rogers says baseball players probably experiment with the drug more than other groups because they see so many players on TV dipping.

"But the popularity nationally has kind of dwindled, I don't see as many Major League Baseball players dipping now as I used to," he said. "I hope that will kind of filter down."

If members of the youth advisory board see baseball players dipping this year, they are encouraged to speak out.

"Imagine the impact that will make, if students went to the principal and complained about that," Hudson said. "I would venture to guess that has never happened before."

4

Teens Swapping Cigarettes for Flavored Mini Cigars

Lena H. Sun

Lena H. Sun is a reporter for The Washington Post.

In recent years, more teens are trading cigarettes for flavored mini cigars and cigarillos, which are cheaper and presumed to be less addictive. Nonetheless, they contain the same cancer-causing agents, and the flavors—including strawberry, watermelon, vanilla, and chocolate—mask the harshness of smoking tobacco. Teens who smoke them state that mini cigars help them cope with stress, are part of socializing, and are sometimes used to smoke marijuana. In some states, their use among adolescents has surpassed that of cigarettes. Some critics accuse the tobacco industry of targeting teens with these products to undermine the ban on flavored cigarettes, but cigar producers insist their products are intended for adults, and that they have used flavors for decades.

They come in ice cream flavors such as strawberry, watermelon, vanilla and chocolate. They are packaged in colorful wrappers. "Little cigars" are finding a niche among teens, who like the price—about a dollar—and the taste.

Young smokers say these cigarette-size little cigars and cigarillos—slimmer versions of big cigars—look better and can be bought one at a time instead of spending more than $5 for a pack of cigarettes. Many teens also think that they are less addictive.

That's a problem.

"You have the same cancer-causing chemicals but wrapped in flavors that don't let you experience the harsh sensation of cigar or tobacco use," said Donald Shell, interim director for Maryland's Center for Health Promotion, Education, Tobacco Use Prevention and Cessation.

Maryland is one of several states where the increase in youth cigar smoking has been large enough that it has caught up with and in some cases surpassed cigarette use in that age group, according to state and federal health data and anti-tobacco groups.

To fight back, the state will launch ads on billboards, buses and trains starting next week [December 2011]. The home page of the campaign Web site, thecigartrap.com, shows youngsters running to an ice cream truck with a giant cigar on its roof. "No matter how they sugarcoat it . . . cigars kill," a warning reads.

Little cigars look like cigarettes but are wrapped in a brown paperlike substance that contains some tobacco leaf.

The Food and Drug Administration banned flavored cigarettes in 2009, but no such ban applies to cigars. Selling tobacco products to anyone younger than 18 is illegal, but not all stores check identification.

Appealing on Several Levels

Some teens and young adults said the smaller cigars were appealing on several levels. Several said the most popular brand is Black & Mild, whose cigarillos come in wine and creme in addition to regular flavors.

Marcus Hunter, 18, said he started smoking cigarillos when he was 14 or 15. "I thought it would help me with stress, you know, from school and stuff," said Hunter during a brief interview outside the Gallery Place Metro station in the District. Hunter, who attended Potomac High School in Oxon Hill, said he stopped smoking a year ago.

Nick Beirne, 20, said he started smoking cigarillos when he turned 18. "It's a social thing," said Beirne, who said he smokes them once or twice a week. A graduate of Yorktown High School in Arlington County, he said teens smoke them "because they think they're less addictive, it looks better and it's cheaper" than cigarettes.

Between 2000 and 2010, cigarette smoking decreased by nearly 40 percent among Maryland high school students, but cigar use jumped more than 11 percent.

A 21-year-old who spoke on the condition of anonymity said that when he was at Calvert High School in Prince Frederick, he and many of his friends thought "the whole cigar thing was way more big to smoke pot," explaining how brands like Swisher Sweets and Black & Mild would be hollowed out and filled with marijuana.

Between 2000 and 2010, cigarette smoking decreased by nearly 40 percent among Maryland high school students, but cigar use jumped more than 11 percent, according to the Maryland Youth Tobacco Survey, a survey of high school students conducted every two years.

In 2000, 23 percent of Maryland high school students younger than 18 reported smoking cigarettes in the previous 30 days, compared with 12.5 percent for cigars, the data show. By 2010, the percentage smoking cigarettes fell to 14.1 percent, and the percentage smoking cigars rose to 13.9 percent. In other words, officials said, almost as many youth smoke cigars as smoke cigarettes.

Nationally, cigar smoking is the second-most-common form of tobacco use among youth, after cigarettes, according to the Centers for Disease Control and Prevention [CDC]. About 14 percent of high school students smoke cigars (18.6 percent among boys; 8.8 percent among girls), according to 2009 CDC data.

More Popular than Cigarette Smoking

But in some states, cigar smoking among some youth groups is more popular than cigarette smoking. In Massachusetts, 18 percent of high school boys smoke cigarettes, but 22 percent smoke cigars, according to 2009 CDC data. A study in Ohio found cigars to be the most popular tobacco product among high school students. In New Jersey, researchers found cigarette use dropped by 29 percent between 2001 and 2004, but for the first time ever, more high school boys reported smoking cigars (17.2 percent) than cigarettes (15.9 percent).

Experts say most states have considerably lower taxes on cigars than on cigarettes. The rise in youth cigar use in New Jersey occurred during a period when the state increased cigarette excise tax three times while the tax on other tobacco products was cut in 2002 from 48 percent to 30 percent, according to researchers at the School of Public Health at the University of Medicine and Dentistry of New Jersey.

The larger issue, according to Matthew Myers, president of the Campaign for Tobacco-Free Kids, "is real concern that tobacco manufacturers are using little cigars to undermine the impact of the federal ban on flavored cigarettes."

The Cigar Association of America, which represents major cigar manufacturers, said in a statement that its members sell a legal product for adults, advocate against youth usage and have used flavors for more than 100 years. The state health campaign, it said, "unfairly maligns an industry that provides jobs and generates tax revenue in Maryland."

5

Quitting Smoking Is as Difficult for Teens as for Adults

David Orenstein

David Orenstein is science news officer of medicine, life sciences, and public health at Brown University.

Teens who are in the early stages of tobacco addiction share many of the withdrawal symptoms of adults, a 2012 study finds. In controlled experiments, adolescent smokers between thirteen and nineteen years old (who, on average, had smoked for two years and had nine cigarettes a day) experienced the urge to smoke, negative changes in mood, and higher provoked cravings in one day of abstinence at levels that were similar to adults who abstained from tobacco. Ultimately, the study's researchers hope that the findings can be used to improve the effectiveness of smoking cessation programs for teens.

Abstinence from smoking seems to affect teens differently than adults in a couple of ways, but a new study provides evidence that most of the psychological difficulties of quitting are as strong for relatively new, young smokers as they are for adults who have been smoking much longer.

"Adolescents are showing—even relatively early in the dependence process—significant, strong, negative effects just after acute abstinence from smoking," said L. Cinnamon Bidwell, assistant professor (research) in psychiatry and human behavior at the Center for Alcohol and Addiction Studies. "Our study shows what those specific effects are. We chose a broad array" of factors to study.

In controlled experiments, teens who abstained for nearly a day experienced withdrawal symptoms, smoking urges, exaccrbations of negative mood, and higher provoked cravings at levels similar to those previously measured in abstaining adults, according to the study published online Sept. 4 [2012] in the journal *Nicotine and Tobacco Research*. Teens who abstained did differ from adults on two measures however: They didn't become more irritated by certain test sounds and they didn't lose the capacity to still feel happy ("positive affect" in the study's parlance).

What the researchers observed . . . was not that abstaining teens have an elevated level of craving when shown smoking cues versus neutral ones, but that their craving level is elevated almost regardless of experimental cues.

"In terms of the subjective negative reactions and the urge reactions, their patterns look remarkably similar to adults," said Suzanne Colby, associate professor (research) in psychiatry and human behavior at the center. "That is really interesting because they are smoking fewer cigarettes per day and they've just been smokers for a shorter period of time."

To conduct the research, lead author Bidwell, senior author Colby, and their team measured a variety of psychological effects on 96 teens aged 13 to 19 in three experimental groups: 22 nonsmokers, 47 smokers whom they asked to abstain for almost a full day, and 27 smokers whom they allowed to continue smoking. On average the teen smokers coming into the study consumed about nine cigarettes a day and had been smoking for about two years.

The researchers made the psychological measurements using standardized methods at two sessions with each group. For the abstainers the first session occurred before abstention and the second occurred during it. The researchers measured the smokers' expired carbon monoxide levels in breath samples at the first session to establish a baseline and again at the second session to confirm whether abstinence, or continued smoking, had indeed occurred.

Confounding Cravings

Among the team's findings was the surprising degree to which abstaining teens felt cravings even when presented with supposedly neutral cues. Their measured craving levels, even when "provoked" with cues as innocuous as a pencil and pad of paper, were about as high as when they were shown overt smoking cues, such as a lit cigarette of their favorite brand.

"They came in and their craving and negative affect were already high," Colby said.

What the researchers observed, therefore, was not that abstaining teens have an elevated level of craving when shown smoking cues versus neutral ones, but that their craving level is elevated almost regardless of experimental cues. But when the researchers compared abstainers to peers who either don't smoke at all, or who didn't have to stop smoking, the abstainers did exhibit a stronger "peak" reaction from smoking-specific cues than the other teens did.

Teen Treatment

Ultimately, Bidwell and Colby hope the research will inform efforts to make smoking cessation and withdrawal treatment more effective for teens. Would it help, they ask, if treatment tried to mitigate these measurable difficulties of abstaining?

"Our findings point to withdrawal, urge (both un-cued and peak provoked), and negative affect (both un-cued and peak provoked) as candidate mediators for treatment efficacy in adolescents and suggest that future treatment trials should be designed to test mediation through these mechanisms," the authors wrote. "It remains unclear whether the lack of efficacy emerges because these treatments do not effectively reduce abstinence effects or, alternatively, because the theoretical approach is incorrect (e.g. these treatments are effective at reducing abstinence effects but reducing the negative effects of abstinence does not improve cessation outcomes)."

But now researchers have a better understanding of what those negative effects of abstinence are for teens; most of those negative effects are just as intense for young, new smokers as for older, more experienced ones.

6

Tobacco Marketing Influences Teen Smoking

Center for Public Health and Tobacco Policy

A project of the Center for Law and Social Responsibility, the Center for Public Health and Tobacco Policy provides policy support and other resources to the New York and Vermont tobacco control communities.

Evidence strongly and consistently points to the influence of tobacco marketing—the intentional promotion and advertising of tobacco products to teens—on youth smoking. According to the scientific data, adolescents are routinely exposed to cigarette advertising in convenience stores and other locations. Adolescents perceive such ads as appealing, and advertisements serve to heighten adolescents' urges to smoke. Furthermore, various studies show that smoking initiation and prevalence among adolescents are related to point-of-sale marketing of cigarettes, as well as to the location and density of stores selling tobacco products. Also, displays and product packaging exposure is associated with youths' increased intentions to smoke. The research even suggests that children are more responsive to tobacco advertising appeals than are adults.

Since the 1994 Surgeon General's report, considerable evidence has accumulated that supports a causal association between marketing efforts of tobacco companies and the initiation and progression of tobacco use among young

Center for Public Health and Tobacco Policy, *Cause and Effect: Tobacco Marketing Increases Youth Tobacco Use*, May 12, 2012. All material quoted from Preventing Tobacco Use Among Youth and Young Adults: A Report of the Surgeon General, 2012.

people. . . . This body of evidence consistently and coherently points to the intentional marketing of tobacco products to youth as being a cause of young people's tobacco use.

Advertising and promotional activities by tobacco companies have been shown to cause the onset and continuation of smoking among adolescents and young adults.

[P]romotion and advertising by the tobacco industry *causes* tobacco use, including its initiation among youth. This conclusion has been buttressed by a multitude of scientific and governmental reports, and the strength of the evidence for causality continues to grow.

A 2003 systematic review of the published longitudinal studies on the impact of advertising concluded "that tobacco advertising and promotion increases the likelihood that adolescents will start to smoke." Both the industry's own internal documents and its testimony in court proceedings, as well as widely accepted principles of advertising and marketing, also support the conclusion that tobacco advertising recruits new users during their youth.

There is strong and consistent evidence that marketing influences adolescent smoking behavior, including selection of brands, initiation of smoking, and overall consumption of cigarettes.

Marketing Influences Youth Smoking Awareness and Behavior

There is strong empirical evidence that tobacco companies' advertising and promotions affect awareness of smoking and of particular brands, the recognition and recall of cigarette advertising, attitudes about smoking, intentions to smoke, and actual smoking behavior. In fact, children appear to be even more responsive to advertising appeals than are adults.

In addition, industry marketing efforts directed at young adults, which are permitted under the [Master Settlement Agreement], have indirect spillover effects on youth through young adults who are aspirational role models for youth.

There is extensive scientific data showing (1) adolescents are regularly exposed to cigarette advertising, (2) they find many of these advertisements appealing, (3) advertisements tend to make smoking appealing, and (4) advertisements serve to increase adolescents' desire to smoke.

There is strong and consistent evidence that marketing influences adolescent smoking behavior, including selection of brands, initiation of smoking, and overall consumption of cigarettes.

[Research] findings suggest that after the Master Settlement Agreement, cigarette advertising continues to reach adolescents, that adolescents continue to be responsive to cigarette advertising, and that those who are responsive are more likely to initiate smoking.

NCI's [National Cancer Institute's] tobacco control monograph, *The Role of the Media in Promoting and Reducing Tobacco Use*, also examined the evidence on how tobacco marketing efforts affect tobacco use among adolescents. Using numerous studies and tobacco industry documents, the report concluded that even brief exposure to tobacco advertising influences attitudes and perceptions about smoking and adolescents' intentions to smoke. In addition, the evidence showed that exposure to cigarette advertising influences non-smoking adolescents to begin smoking and move toward regular smoking.

The continuously accumulating evidence from the studies that have addressed the effect of advertising on smoking is consistent with a dose-dependent causal relationship.[1]

---

1. A dose-dependent relationship means that the impact of tobacco advertising is directly linked to the amount of exposure to such advertising.

Taking together the epidemiology of adolescent tobacco use, internal tobacco company documents describing the importance of new smokers, analysis of the design of marketing campaigns, the actual imagery communicated in the $10-billion-a-year marketing effort, the conclusions of official government reports, and the weight of the scientific evidence, it is concluded that advertising and promotion has caused youth to start smoking and continue to smoke.

[D]espite claims from cigarette manufacturers that marketing and promotion of their products are intended to increase market share and promote brand loyalty among adult consumers, the evidence presented in this [viewpoint] is sufficient to conclude that marketing efforts and promotion by tobacco companies show a consistent dose-response relationship in the initiation and progression of tobacco use among young people.

Point-of-Sale Marketing Increases Youth Tobacco Use

[A] longitudinal study of more than 1,600 adolescents aged 11–14 years found that the odds of initiating smoking more than doubled for adolescents reporting that they visited the types of stores that contain the most cigarette advertising (convenience stores, liquor stores, and small grocery stores) two or more times a week. [The study controlled for] risk factors typically associated with uptake of smoking such as smoking by family and friends.

A systematic review of eight cross-sectional studies on the impact of tobacco promotion at the point of sale consistently found significant associations between exposure to point-of-sale tobacco promotions and initiation of smoking or susceptibility to that behavior. In conclusion, tobacco marketing at the point of sale is associated with the use of tobacco by youth. Because point-of-sale marketing is an important channel for the tobacco companies, with very few restrictions, consumers, including children, are unavoidably exposed to pro-smoking messages when they shop or when they are simply passing by stores.

The presence of heavy cigarette advertising in [convenience] stores has been shown to increase the likelihood of exposing youth to prosmoking messages, which can increase initiation rates among those exposed.

Location of Retail Stores

Neighborhoods that are more densely populated with stores selling tobacco may promote adolescent smoking not only by increasing access but also by increasing environmental cues to smoke.

In Chicago, Illinois, youth in areas with the highest density of retail tobacco outlets were 13% more likely to have smoked in the past month than those living in areas with the lowest density of outlets. In a California study, the prevalence of current smoking was higher in high schools with the highest density of tobacco outlets in their neighborhoods than in high schools in neighborhoods without any outlets; the density of retail cigarette advertising in school neighborhoods was also associated with smoking prevalence.

The presence of heavy cigarette advertising in [convenience] stores has been shown to increase the likelihood of exposing youth to prosmoking messages, which can increase initiation rates among those exposed, particularly if stores are near schools.

[R]esearch on the location of retail outlets selling cigarettes indicated that experimental smoking among youth was related to the density of tobacco outlets both in high school neighborhoods and in neighborhoods where youth live.

Tobacco Product Displays and Packaging

The brand imagery on cigarette packages is effective to the point that large majorities of youth—including nonsmoking youth demonstrate high levels of recall for leading package designs.

Two studies conducted in countries that ban cigarette advertising at the point of sale confirm that exposure of adolescents to pack displays is associated with increased intentions to smoke among youth.

[I]n two experimental studies, students who saw photos of stores with tobacco displays and advertising were more likely to overestimate the percentage of adolescents and adults who smoke and to believe that tobacco is easier to buy than were those who saw photos without retail tobacco materials.

Recent research suggests that even when terms such as "light" and "mild" are prohibited in tobacco packaging and advertising, a significant proportion of adult and youth smokers continue to report false beliefs about the relative risk of cigarette brands. Studies suggest that the use of lighter colors on cigarette packs to imply lightness, as well as replacement words such as "smooth," have the same misleading effect as "light" and "mild" labels.

Price Promotions That Reduce the Cost of Tobacco Products

[Y]outh respond more than adults to price changes in terms of their use of tobacco.

Given the greater price sensitivity of smoking among young people . . . the industry's targeted pricing and price-reducing promotion strategies will have their greatest impact on youth and young adults.

[A] growing and increasingly sophisticated body of research has clearly demonstrated that tobacco use among young people is responsive to changes in the prices of tobacco products. Most of these studies have found that usage levels among young people change more in response to price changes than do usage levels among adults. This research includes studies that have looked at the consumption of cigarettes and smokeless tobacco products as well as various stages of cigarette smoking among youth and young adults.

In considering the numerous studies demonstrating that tobacco use among young people is responsive to changes in the prices of tobacco products, it can be concluded that the industry's extensive use of price-reducing promotions has led to higher rates of tobacco use among young people than would have occurred in the absence of these promotions.

7

Antismoking Campaigns Can Be Effective with Teens

Michele R. Berman

Michele R. Berman is a physician and cofounder of Celebrity Diagnosis, www.celebritydiagnosis.com, a website focusing on issues in medicine and health.

Antismoking campaigns that show the serious health consequences of cigarette use in graphic or extreme ways can influence teens. To be effective, such a "fear campaign" needs to also elicit disgust, which is proven to portray smoking as undesirable and immoral. Disgust is key—it is the reaction to an immoral act, encouraging action to end or eradicate smoking. Adolescents, moreover, fall into two groups: promotion-oriented (motivated by benefits and responsive to positive messages) and prevention-oriented (motivated by protection and responsive to negative messages). These differences in teen viewers should be considered in improving antismoking campaigns.

What would it take to make you stop smoking? Or to keep you from ever starting?

The Centers for Disease Control and Prevention (CDC) is hoping that a new $54 million ad campaign, which began this week [March 2012], will do just that.

This campaign is different than most "don't do this, it's bad for you" ads. It is designed to gross you out, make you cringe and/or shock you to quit smoking or never start in the first place.

The campaign, called "Tips From Former Smokers," uses stories and graphic pictures of ex-smokers who have suffered the dire consequences of smoking addiction. One features a 50-year-old man from Washington state who has to shave around the gaping hole in his neck through which he has to breathe. It sports the caption: "Be careful not to cut your stoma!"

Another shows a 31-year-old putting on his prosthetic legs, the result of Buerger's Disease that he's had since age 18. Buerger's Disease is a vasculitis of the small arteries and veins of the hands and feet. Thrombi can lead to necrosis and amputations. It is strongly associated with cigarette smoking, especially in young men ages 20–40 years old.

Department of Health and Human Services (DHHS) Secretary Kathleen Sebelius said in a statement:

> Hundreds of thousands of lives are lost each year due to smoking, and for every person who dies, 20 more Americans live with an illness caused by smoking. . . . We cannot afford to continue watching the human and economic toll from tobacco rob our communities of parents and grandparents, aunts and uncles, friends and co-workers. We are committed to doing everything we can to help smokers quit and prevent young people from starting in the first place.

Shocking Facts About Smoking and Adolescents

According to the U.S. Surgeon General, Vice Admiral Regina Benjamin, MD:

Today, more than 600,000 middle school students and 3 million high school students smoke cigarettes.

Rates of decline for cigarette smoking have slowed in the last decade, and rates of decline for smokeless tobacco use have stalled completely.

Every day, more than 1,200 people in this country die due to smoking. For each of those deaths, at least two youth or young adults become regular smokers each day.

Almost 90% of those replacement smokers smoke their first cigarette by age 18.

There could be 3 million fewer young smokers today if success in reducing youth tobacco use that was made between 1997 and 2003 had been sustained.

Nearly 9 out of 10 smokers started smoking by age 18, and 99% started by age 26.

Rates of smokeless tobacco use are no longer declining, and they appear to be increasing among some groups.

Cigars, especially cigarette-sized cigars, are popular with youth. One out of five high school males smokes cigars, and cigar use appears to be increasing among other groups.

Use of multiple tobacco products—including cigarettes, cigars, and smokeless tobacco—is common among young people.

Prevention efforts must focus on young adults ages 18 through 25, too. Almost no one starts smoking after age 25. Nearly 9 out of 10 smokers started smoking by age 18, and 99% started by age 26. Progression from occasional to daily smoking almost always occurs by age 26.

Do Disgusting Ads Really Work?
Yeah, Sort Of

There have certainly been some successful anti-smoking campaigns in the past:

Those that aired in the late 1960s helped drive a 10% decline in cigarette consumption from 1967 to 1970.

In the early 2000s the American Legacy Foundation launched its "truth" ads. It was the largest national youth smoking prevention campaign not directed by the tobacco industry itself.

"[T]ruth" provided facts and information about tobacco products and the tobacco industry, and gave teens tools to enable them to take control and make informed decisions about tobacco use. The ads are credited with a large drop in youth smoking at the time.

But recent studies say that it's not just the message, but how that message is presented that's important.

Cornelia (Connie) Pechmann, MBA, PhD, a researcher at the University of California Irvine, has extensively studied just this. In her 2006 article, she says that "fear campaigns" can work well with adolescents, but they need to provoke more than fear—they need to provoke disgust! Health appeals need not evoke fear, though; they may evoke disgust. Research indicates that associating smoking with disgust is perhaps the single most effective way to make smoking socially unacceptable and encourage anti-smoking activism. Disgust is what people feel in response to an immoral act, and it motivates action. Whereas fear is associated with a desire to escape or hide, disgust is associated with a desire to expel or obliterate.

Researchers also suggest tailoring ad campaigns to target teens with different motivational priorities.

Are You Promotion- or Prevention-Oriented?

Most adolescents seem to belong to one of two groups: those who are promotion-oriented, and those who are prevention-oriented.

The promotion-oriented group thinks in terms of "How will this benefit me and get me ahead?" while the prevention-oriented group thinks "How can I protect myself from this?"

Promotion-focused teens respond best to positive messages, while prevention focused teens react more strongly to negative messages.

In 2007, [researchers Guangzhi] Zhao and [Connie] Pechmann studied how these differences can be used to improve the impact of anti-smoking advertisements. They concluded that ads can be enhanced by "aligning the message's regulatory focus [orientation] and the message frame to viewers' regulatory focus." For promotion-focused adolescents, a promotion-focused positively framed anti-smoking advertisement about attaining social approval was effective at persuading them not to smoke. For prevention-focused adolescents, a prevention-focused negatively framed anti-smoking advertisement about incurring social disapproval was effective at persuading them not to smoke. Advertisers need to take this into consideration when designing anti-smoking campaigns. Considering the tobacco industry spends $10 billion a year to promote their product, anti-smoking forces need all the help they can get.

8

Antismoking Campaigns from Tobacco Companies Are Purposely Ineffective

Ann Boonn

Ann Boonn is associate director at the Campaign for Tobacco-Free Kids, a nonprofit organization based in Washington, DC.

Instead of preventing teen smoking or encouraging smokers to quit, antismoking campaigns launched by tobacco companies are designed to promote smoking, fend off regulation, and influence the public and policy makers. Studies have proven that these campaigns are not only ineffective but also act to lower perceptions of tobacco's dangers and subtly encourage teens to smoke. In fact, many of these refusal and "choice" ads have no impact on prevention and actually boost the image and brand of tobacco companies, countering antismoking efforts. Additionally, expenditures for antismoking campaigns are dwarfed by the massive amounts companies spend on marketing their products as well as combating tobacco taxes, cigarette bans, and other measures that effectively reduce smoking.

For decades, tobacco companies have launched their own so-called youth prevention campaigns virtually every time they are faced with legislation, regulation, or litigation that they know will reduce smoking. Their latest campaigns aimed at youth and parents are simply the latest incarnation of thinly disguised public relations efforts to influence public opinion and policy makers rather than smoking behavior.

After years of these efforts, three things are quite clear:

- No tobacco company campaign has EVER produced any evidence that it prevents kids from smoking or helps smokers quit. In fact, evidence from several recent studies confirms that these programs are ineffective at best and even work to ENCOURAGE kids to smoke.

- The goals of the industry campaigns are not to reduce smoking, and the targets of the campaigns are not kids or smokers. The tobacco companies' own documents reveal that these campaigns are merely part of their ongoing efforts to convince policy makers NOT to enact those policies and programs that actually reduce tobacco use.

- While foisting these fake prevention campaigns on the public, the tobacco companies have dramatically increased their marketing expenditures that promote smoking, much of it in ways that influence youth to smoke. They spend additional untold millions to oppose tobacco taxes, smoke-free laws, and funding for tobacco prevention programs, all of which are proven to reduce smoking among youth and adults and/or protect everyone from the harms of secondhand smoke.

Evidence That Industry-Funded Prevention Programs Are Ineffective at Best, Harmful at Worst

Research studies show that tobacco companies' campaigns don't prevent youth from smoking.

- A study published in 2009 found that youth who recalled Philip Morris' "Think. Don't Smoke" advertisements had more favorable beliefs and attitudes towards cigarette companies, and those beliefs increased even after that campaign went off-air. In addition, youth recalling the industry ads were less likely to say that they would not smoke within the next year.

Industry ads that use a "choice" theme and focus on refusal messages appear to have no effect on preventing smoking initiation, do not resonate with teens, and do not appear to offer any compelling reason not to smoke.

- A 2006 study published in the *American Journal of Public Health* found that the industry's "prevention" ads targeted at youth are ineffective and do not change smoking outcomes, while industry ads targeted at parents increase the likelihood that kids will smoke. Among 10th and 12th graders, higher exposure to the parent-targeted ads was associated with lower perceived harm of smoking, stronger approval of smoking, stronger intentions to smoke in the future, and a greater likelihood of having smoked in the past 30 days.

- In an exhaustive review of relevant studies, a comprehensive report released in June 2008 by the National Cancer Institute, *The Role of the Media in Promoting and Reducing Tobacco Use*, confirmed that tobacco industry-sponsored youth smoking prevention programs are "generally ineffective" at reducing youth smoking and may have caused some youth to start smoking.

- A systematic review of mass media campaigns on youth smoking published in 2008, found that tobacco industry-funded youth prevention campaigns have minimal impact on youth smoking because they avoid the most powerful anti-tobacco themes of health effects and industry manipulation. Industry youth prevention media campaigns that position smoking as an adult habit or as a "choice" and ignore the consequences of smoking are not effective, and in fact may undermine the effects of aggressive media campaigns. Industry ads that use a "choice" theme and focus on refusal messages appear to have no effect on preventing smoking initiation, do not resonate with teens, and do not appear to offer any compelling reason not to smoke. The 2008 review found that tobacco industry youth prevention campaigns may actually undermine tobacco control efforts because they improve the tobacco industry's public image.

- Researchers found that youth exposed to Philip Morris' "Think. Don't Smoke" advertisements had more favorable feelings toward the tobacco industry compared to youth who were not exposed to the ads. This finding supports the assertion that the purpose of this campaign was not to prevent youth smoking, but rather to buy respectability and favor among youth.

- Lorillard heavily promoted its "youth smoking prevention" campaign, "Tobacco is Whacko . . . If You're A Teen," despite lack of evidence that it has ever had any impact whatsoever on teens. The "Tobacco is Whacko . . . If You're A Teen" slogan framed smoking as an adult activity, which, as tobacco industry documents recognize, is an effective way to appeal to kids and can tempt teens to try smoking.

- Experts expressed serious concerns that the manner in which the "Tobacco is Whacko" campaign was framed encouraged young people to smoke as an act of rebellion rather than discouraging tobacco use.

- A 2000 study by the California Department of Health Services showed that the much publicized "We Card" program, promoted by the tobacco industry as a voluntary means to keep underage kids from purchasing tobacco products, had little or no effect on underage tobacco sales. The California data for 1998 and 1999 demonstrated that the rate of illegal underage sales for stores with "We Card" and other tobacco industry signs was much higher than stores with government signs prohibiting illegal sales to minors; compliance increased only when the tobacco industry signs were coupled with government signs.

Judge's Opinion Reiterates That Tobacco Companies' Prevention Programs Are Ineffective

In her landmark opinion in 2006, finding the tobacco companies guilty of lying to the American people and marketing their deadly and addictive products to our children, Judge [Gladys] Kessler was very specific in finding that industry youth prevention programs have no merit. According to Judge Kessler:

- "Defendants never recommend that parents inform their children that smoking kills more than 400,000 people each year, involves an addiction that most smokers desire to end, and will harm those around the smoker. Nor do Defendants ever suggest that parents, as role models for their children, stop smoking."

- "Defendants' 'youth programs' and youth smoking prevention efforts are not only minimally funded— given the vast sums they spend on marketing and promotion to youth—and understaffed both quali- tatively and quantitatively, but no efforts have been made to validate their effectiveness amongst the total population."

- "[B]oth Lorillard's and Philip Morris's media cam- paigns promote the message that smoking is an adult decision. Emphasizing that smoking is an adult activity underscores the desirability of engag- ing in adult behavior for adolescents who are par- ticularly motivated to appear mature."

Tobacco companies launch youth anti-smoking cam- paigns as public relations efforts to discourage regulation and public action to reduce smoking.

Even Advertising Critics See Through Tobacco Companies' Youth Prevention Campaigns

- *ADWEEK* columnist Barbara Lippert wrote: "[T]hese ads are too tepid and generic—they could sell anything from orange juice to toothpaste. . . . PM [Philip Morris] has chosen to create a mellow, sensitive, 'rely on your good sense, son' picture. Are they serious? This is advertising covering a life-and-death issue! So where is the big stick? The scare tactics? The hit 'em over your head with destroying life stuff?"

- *USA Today* advertising columnist Bruce Horovitz placed Philip Morris' new campaign on his "Worst Ads of 1998" list. He wrote: "This is Philip Morris' jaded attempt at PR. Three spots with kids who say smoking isn't cool. . . . Philip Morris says it wants kids to stop smoking. Right. Just like Bill Gates wants kids to stop staring at computer screens."

- Fred Goldberg, chairman-CEO of Goldberg Moser O'Neill, an advertising agency in San Francisco, wrote in *Advertising Age*: "I call it unmitigated gall and hypocrisy; incredible and disheartening. It is another reflection of the distorted values and warped standards that exist today more than ever."

If tobacco companies really wanted to reduce youth smoking, they would stop their aggressive marketing tactics and stop opposing the policies and programs that actually work to reduce smoking.

The Real Reason Tobacco Companies Have Youth Prevention Campaigns

Tobacco companies launch youth anti-smoking campaigns as public relations efforts to discourage regulation and public action to reduce smoking, such as litigation or legislation, with the goal to improve their public image and reduce opportunities for opponents to impose restraints on industry practices. Their targets, then, are not youths or parents of youths, but policymakers and the general public. It is likely that a key motivation is to discourage Congress and state legislatures from enacting measures such as tobacco taxes, smoke-free laws, and funding for tobacco prevention and cessation programs that they know and that sciences tells us will reduce smoking among both youth and adults.

- From Judge Kessler's Final Opinion. "Internal documents suggest that Defendants designed their YSP [youth smoking prevention] programs for public relations rather than efficacy in youth smoking prevention."

- From a 1991 Tobacco Institute discussion paper: "The youth [anti-smoking] program and its individual parts support the Institute's objective of discouraging unfair and counterproductive federal, state, and local restrictions on cigarette advertising, by: (a) providing on-going and persuasive evidence that the industry is actively discouraging youth smoking and independent verification that the industry's efforts are valid; (b) Reinforcing the belief that peer pressure—not advertising—is the cause of youth smoking [and] (c) Seizing the political center and forcing the antismokers to an extreme."

- In a 1995 draft speech, Philip Morris President and CEO Joseph J. Morgan stated, "The bottom line to all this is, I repeat, if we don't do something fast to project that sense of industry responsibility regarding the youth access issue, we are going to be looking at severe marketing restrictions in a very short time. Those restrictions will pave the way for equally severe legislation or regulation on where adults are allowed to smoke. We need to do something to demonstrate industry agreement, concern and action on the youth-access issue. . . ."

- From a 1992 Philip Morris document: "[If Philip Morris took] a more progressive position on tobacco, it would enable the company to move onto a higher moral playing field, to neutralize the tobacco issue and to focus attention on other, more appealing products."

The Industry Continues to Market Its Products Aggressively

As noted previously, marketing by tobacco companies has increased dramatically since the tobacco settlement, reaching a record $12.8 billion per year—$35.2 million a day—in 2006 (the most recent year for which complete data is available). If tobacco companies really wanted to reduce youth smoking, they would stop their aggressive marketing tactics and stop opposing the policies and programs that actually work to reduce smoking.

- Judge Kessler stated, "Philip Morris continues to increase its marketing expenditures in grossly disproportionate amounts to its spending on youth smoking prevention. Philip Morris's 2003 Financial Forecast Budget includes a budget of $110 million for youth smoking prevention, $8.9 million greater than its 2002 spending, 'primarily due to increased spending for adult cessation programs.' In contrast, in that year, Philip Morris spent more than $7.1 billion on sales incentives and product promotions."

- According to the Federal Trade Commission (FTC), in 2003, cigarette companies increased their product marketing and promotional spending to $15.15 billion, while lowering their spending on youth smoking prevention programs to $72.9 million. In other words, tobacco companies spent more than 200 times on product marketing than on prevention.

Tobacco Companies Continue to Oppose Real Prevention Programs and Other Policies That Reduce Smoking

The 2008 NCI [National Cancer Institute] report on tobacco use and the media describes the great lengths the tobacco industry will go to influence tobacco control media interventions. Tobacco companies obstruct state anti-tobacco media campaigns by lobbying elected officials to reduce or eliminate funding for these programs, by attempting to weaken the campaign messages or reduce the size of their target audiences and by arguing that state anti-tobacco media campaigns are a waste of taxpayer dollars because they duplicate the industry's own tobacco prevention campaigns—which, as proven above, are ineffective.

Below are a few examples of major efforts by tobacco companies to thwart tobacco control measures at the ballot.

- According to state campaign contribution reports, in 2006, Philip Morris, R.J. Reynolds and other tobacco interests spent at least $70.1 million in California and Missouri to oppose state ballot initiatives that would use revenues from a tobacco tax increase to fund proven-effective state youth prevention programs. The industry's money bought a barrage of deceptive television ads that misled voters about the impact of these initiatives, going so far as to claim that the initiatives did not provide enough money for tobacco prevention when in fact they would have given California and Missouri two of the best-funded tobacco prevention programs in the country.

- In 2006, tobacco companies launched a major effort to thwart a proposed $1-a-pack increase on the state cigarette tax in Texas. Philip Morris and R.J. Reynolds conducted an anti-tax campaign that consisted of radio commercials, newspaper ads and computer-generated phone calls to lawmakers. In addition, according to Texans for Public Justice, which monitors lobby influence in Austin, tobacco companies spent at least $1.4 million lobbying the state legislature against the tax increase.

- In 2006, R.J. Reynolds spent $7.1 million in Arizona to deter voters from supporting a ballot initiative that would make bars smoke-free and another $5.4 million towards defeating a similar ballot initiative in Ohio. Voters rejected these multi-million dollar campaigns by the tobacco industry and sent a loud and clear message to elected officials at all levels: Reject the special interests of the tobacco industry and protect the public interest by supporting proven measures to reduce tobacco use and exposure to secondhand smoke.

- In 2007, tobacco industries spent a record $12 million—or $24 per vote—to defeat a ballot initiative to raise Oregon's tobacco tax and fund health care for uninsured children.

9

Debating Age Limits on Tobacco

Nicholas Bakalar

Based in New York, Nicholas Bakalar is a writer and author with a focus on health, medicine, and science. He regularly contributes to the Well *blog published by* The New York Times.

Raising the age limits on the purchase of tobacco is touted as an effective way to reduce teen smoking. The scientific data, however, on such age restrictions remains unclear, and concrete evidence is elusive. For instance, a study claims that raising the minimum age from sixteen to eighteen to buy tobacco in Britain reduced smoking among students ages eleven to fifteen. But it did not include sixteen and seventeen year-olds, the group most impacted. In addition, a study of Massachusetts teens and smoking laws concluded that different restrictions and levels of enforcement did not impact smoking initiation among the age group.

The New York City Council has taken up a proposal to raise the minimum age for tobacco purchases to 21 from 18, the strictest such limits in any major American city.

Smoking declined significantly among the city's teenagers from 2005 to 2007, then remained level through 2012, and Christine C. Quinn, the City Council speaker, has cited "clear data" showing that 80 percent of smokers begin before age 21.

"We have an ability to intervene on that and make a difference," Ms. Quinn said last week at a news conference last week.

But the scientific picture is a bit murkier than it might seem. While most tobacco researchers agree that age restrictions will do no harm and may well help reduce the incidence of smoking among teenagers, firm scientific proof for their effectiveness is hard to come by.

In 2007, the minimum age for buying tobacco in Britain was raised to 18 from 16. The new limit had some beneficial effect, according to two studies cited by Ms. Quinn and Dr. Thomas A. Farley, the city's health commissioner. In the first, published in October 2011 in the journal *Thorax*, a survey of 7,798 students ages 11 to 15 found that the law reduced the number who reported smoking at least one cigarette a week.

But the data did not include 16- and 17-year-olds, presumably the teenagers most affected by the change. The authors acknowledged that "the sample size did not permit us to examine whether the legislation reduced the volume of cigarettes smoked."

There is some evidence that you can tighten up on [tobacco] sales, but then young people find other sources.

The second British study, published in the November 2010 issue of *Addiction*, also depended on self-reports and found that smoking decreased more in 16- and 17-year olds than in any other age group after implementation of the 2007 law. But smoking decreased in all age groups, the authors noted, suggesting that raising the minimum purchase age could not have been the only factor at work.

One study, published in 2007 in Tobacco Control, was a two-year prospective analysis of a random sample of 2,623 teenagers in Massachusetts; the researchers linked self-reported teenage smoking to a statewide database of smoking laws and enforcement practices.

The study found that varying laws and levels of enforcement made no difference in the rate of teenagers taking up smoking, although the authors acknowledged that other anti-smoking initiatives during the period could have hidden the effect.

Not Completely Convincing

Amanda Amos, a professor of health promotion at the University of Edinburgh who has published widely on teenage smoking, agreed that the data on whether age laws work is not completely convincing.

"When you look at the evidence about whether it actually decreases smoking, that's not so clear," Dr. Amos said. "There is some evidence that you can tighten up on sales, but then young people find other sources."

Dr. Farley is more optimistic. "I would characterize the evidence as quite positive," he said. "The two that are the strongest are the study in England where they showed a big decline, and the data from Needham, which shows a remarkable decline over six years which was not matched here or anywhere else."

Needham, a town in Massachusetts, raised the minimum sale age to 21 in 2005. According to a health survey conducted in 24 high schools in the region, 5.5 percent of Needham students were smokers in 2012, down from 12.9 percent in 2006.

What might account for the varied results in these studies? "A lot of the studies have found that the direct impact depends on enforcement," Dr. Amos said. "The more you put into enforcement, the better it works."

The new law does not change the penalties to retailers for selling to underage customers, nor does it criminalize smoking or the possession of cigarettes by people under 21.

"All studies have their weaknesses," Dr. Farley said. "You can't do randomized controlled trials of a law. The closest you get is where you track over time the thing you expect to change and compare it to the places where you didn't change the law. The data is pretty solid, and it makes all the sense in the world."

10

E-Cigs: Popular With Kids, but What's in Them?

Andrew Schneider

Andrew Schneider is senior public health correspondent for AOL News.

Available in flavors like bubble gum, fudge, and cookie dough, electronic cigarettes are quickly gaining popularity among teens and younger kids. While selling tobacco products to anyone under age eighteen is nationally prohibited, no federal laws exist that ban selling electronic cigarettes to children. And only a few states have age restrictions on the sale of the devices. Especially worrying is that the safety, quality, and effects of electronic cigarettes are still unknown, and emerging research suggests a host of health dangers and irreversible lung damage. Still, the industry remains secretive about information regarding these products, and the US Food and Drug Administration—without yet receiving this information or testing the toxicity of electronic cigarettes—is slow to become involved in regulation.

Two eighth-grade girls carrying their pink cell phones and a tan envelope with cash stopped at a stand in a far corner of the sprawling Union Station in Washington, D.C.

The one-table kiosk offered individual electronic cigarettes for $20 and "complete starter packs" with multiple flavors for

$140. The girls, who had ridden Amtrak from Philadelphia, bought an assortment for themselves and some friends.

"They're very grown-up, you know," one girl said.

There is a nationwide prohibition on selling tobacco products to anyone under 18, but AOL News was unable to find any federal laws that ban the sale of these nicotine-dispersing faux cigarettes to children, despite growing concerns about the safety of the products by health experts and the public.

Only a handful of states, like New Hampshire, Arizona, Oregon, Minnesota and New Jersey, restrict the sale by age. Others are considering restrictions or outright bans. The devices are being advertised and sold to kids and grown-ups throughout the country, yet little is known about what the estimated million or more people using them are sucking into their lungs.

"The sale of these electronic devices is absolutely a health issue, especially to children," Marie Cocco, a spokeswoman for the Campaign for Tobacco-Free Kids, told AOL News this week.

Her fear is that these devices have been and are being sold in hundreds of malls across the U.S. Estimates from the e-cigarettes industry say the number of outlets is probably higher than 500 and growing rapidly.

With e-cigs flavors like bubblegum, buttered popcorn, fudge and cookie dough, and the fact that there is apparently no age restriction on their sale to minors, the devices are becoming enormously popular among teens and even those younger, says the Campaign for Tobacco-Free Kids and other health advocacy groups.

The Food and Drug Administration did go after five e-cigarette companies last week [September 2010] for, among other things, claiming that the devices are a smoking deterrent and can cure erectile dysfunction and lead to weight loss. But critics say the agency has done nothing to halt the sale of the products in the U.S., despite concerns about health effects that led Canada and several other countries to ban them.

[Ninety-one] percent think manufacturers should be required to test e-cigarettes for safety, 85 percent favor prohibiting the sale of e-cigarettes to minors and 82 percent think the FDA should regulate e-cigarettes like other nicotine-containing products.

Survey: Public Wants Regulation

Almost all of the electronic smoking devices—cigarettes, pipes or cigars—contain a metal tube; a rechargeable, battery-operated heating element; a replaceable cartridge that may contain nicotine or other liquids; and an atomizer that, when heated, converts the contents of the cartridge into a smoke-like vapor.

All are designed to deliver vapors of nicotine, flavoring agents or other substances, including vitamins, herbal remedies, "calming ingredients" and medication guaranteed to cure or help almost any ailment.

That may sound innocent enough, but a new study shows that many people are already worried about these untested products.

According to a survey of 2,061 people released this week by the University of Michigan's National Poll on Children's Health, 91 percent think manufacturers should be required to test e-cigarettes for safety, 85 percent favor prohibiting the sale of e-cigarettes to minors and 82 percent think the FDA should regulate e-cigarettes like other nicotine-containing products.

"There is not yet much scientific evidence about e-cigarettes and kids yet, because these new devices have not been tested extensively," Dr. Matthew Davis, director of the University of Michigan C.S. Mott Children's Hospital National Poll on Children's Health, told AOL News. "But our poll results strongly indicate that many adults are worried about e-cigarettes leading kids to smoke tobacco. Most adults feel that e-cigarettes should be regulated by the FDA like other nicotine-containing products."

Do No Harm?

Toxicologists, risk assessors and cancer specialists from the National Institutes of Health, the Centers for Disease Control and Prevention and the FDA have long worried about the hazards that could be caused by using these devices. So why has it taken so long for the FDA to get involved?

The agency says it hasn't tested the toxicity of the liquids or "e-juice" used in the devices or received any useful information from the distributors. Nevertheless, the FDA acknowledges there are signs of health problems.

"FDA is aware of reports of short-term side effects from the use of electronic cigarettes, including racing pulse, dizziness, slurred speech, mouth ulcers, heartburn, coughing, diarrhea and sore throat," FDA spokeswoman Siobhan DeLancey told AOL News. She added that the agency doesn't know how common or potentially serious these effects may be.

The composition and toxicity of the flavoring agents worry some with expertise in the field. One physician who for years has studied the damaging effects of the butter flavoring diacetyl in microwave popcorn factory workers and consumers told AOL News he is concerned about the use of the substance in e-cigarette flavorings.

"It's criminal to allow diacetyl and other untested flavoring agents to be used in these devices," said Dr. David Egilman, clinical associate professor at Brown University's Department of Family Medicine. "At the very least, it's not smart to intentionally inhale substances which have been proven to cause irreversible lung disease that has and can kill you."

For about 10 years, Egilman has served as an expert witness in scores of cases of people allegedly harmed by diacetyl.

"Americans need to understand that contrary to political rhetoric, there is no real federal regulation of food or food additives," he said. "There is overwhelming evidence that smoke from cigarettes which contains diacetyl causes disease in the terminal bronchioles—the furthest and smallest tubes that carry air to the lungs."

Canadians Ban E-cigs, Why Not U.S.?

Health Canada had no more information than the FDA does on these products, but last year the Canadian agency ordered that "persons importing, advertising or selling electronic cigarette products in Canada must stop doing so immediately" because they "may pose health risks and have not been fully evaluated for safety, quality and efficacy" by the agency.

"The prohibition on these electronic cigarettes still stands," Health Canada spokesman Gary Scott Holub told AOL News this week.

What little analysis [of electronic cigarettes] FDA has conducted shows potentially serious problems.

If the Canadians could do it, why not U.S. regulators?

The answer from the FDA's spokeswoman was lacking in specifics and offered no clue as to why the agency didn't take a firmer stand.

"The agency has not made a decision to remove all e-cigarettes from the market," but "will regulate electronic cigarettes and related products in a manner consistent with its mission of protecting the public health," DeLancey said.

What little analysis FDA has conducted shows potentially serious problems.

Agency scientists examined 19 different e-cig brands from two major distributors and found disturbing results, including:

- Significant quality problems that indicate that quality-control processes used to manufacture these products are substandard or nonexistent.

- Cartridges labeled as containing no nicotine contained low levels of nicotine in all tested but one; three different electronic cigarette cartridges with the same label emitted a markedly different amount of nicotine with each puff.

- Certain tobacco-specific nitrosamines, which are human carcinogens, were detected in half of the samples tested.

- Tobacco-specific impurities suspected of being harmful to humans—anabasine, myosmine and β-nicotyrine—were detected in a majority of the samples tested.

As a result of these findings, the FDA greatly angered the industry when it thwarted the importation of more than 800 shipments of electronic cigarettes into the U.S. on the grounds that they were unapproved drug devices. At least two importers roared that the FDA had no right to meddle with their products and quickly filed suit in federal court.

Photographs of attractive young people and beautiful women gazing into the distance are used by most of the online sales sites to convey the message that e-cigs are cool.

Perhaps the lingering lawsuits by two e-cig importers and intense lobbying on Capitol Hill thwarted earlier efforts by U.S. agencies to regulate the products, let alone halt their sale. But last week's FDA action against five large distributors offered some hope that the unfettered marketing of these products may be slowed a bit.

A Secretive Industry

It's difficult for potential regulators, health investigators and even consumers to get direct answers to questions about the industry.

But in May, a man who offered only a first name, which changed from Fedir to Teddy and back, said he was responding to AOL News' request from information from the Electronic Cigarette Association.

Here's what came from scattered discussions with him:

- More than 1.25 million people are using the cigarette products, and between 2,000 and 18,000 new users begin sucking on the metal and plastic devices each month.

- Between 300 and 500 companies are selling the products in the U.S., some running 30 or more separate outlets, but, Fedir added, "only a handful of people own them all."

- The devices were manufactured in five Chinese factories, three owned by the same people, but are sometimes transshipped through European ports.

Photographs of attractive young people and beautiful women gazing into the distance are used by most of the online sales sites to convey the message that e-cigs are cool, Fedir explained.

By far, he said, the greatest sales come from websites and online stores. Importers sell the same e-cigs under various names.

When asked about health studies, Fedir said he would get the information. He never did.

AOL News attempted repeatedly to contact Matt Salmon, who, according to the FDA, is the current president of the industry association to verify and update the information offered four months ago by Fedir. Salmon did not respond to several e-mails, and the phone numbers on the association's website were for a public relations agency that said it was no longer handling "that account."

Concerns Remain, but Who's Paying Attention?

Some of the e-cig websites insist they have corrected problems in their products that FDA scientists reported last year.

"FDA is still concerned about electronic cigarettes because there is little scientific information on their safety, efficacy or quality," DeLancey said.

But the two eighth-grade girls from Philadelphia were oblivious to all that jargon when they made their purchases that day at Union Station in Washington. Why did they travel more than 130 miles each way to buy e-cigarettes?

"They're a lot cheaper here," one of the girls said before they both rushed off to get the train home.

11

For Teenage Smokers, Removing the Allure of the Pack

Tina Rosenberg

Tina Rosenberg is a Pulitzer Prize-winning author and contributing writer to The New York Times *Sunday magazine.*

Teens begin smoking to be cool, lighting up as an act of rebellion against adults. Therefore, the most effective way to prevent teen smoking is to make cigarettes uncool. For example, the anti-smoking campaign "Truth" was successful because it directed teens' yearnings to rebel toward tobacco companies, dramatically cutting the percentage of high school smokers. Another way to remove the appeal of tobacco is to eliminate it from movies, as exposure to such images is strongly associated with smoking initiation. Finally, introducing plain packaging to all cigarette brands also has potential. More than adults, teens smoke the most advertised brands, and cigarettes would lose some cool factor without the labels.

Remember teenage smoking? It's been edged out by teenage obesity as the health concern of the moment. States are cutting programs to prevent the former while establishing programs to combat the latter.

We shouldn't forget about it. Last year [2011], 18.7 percent of high school seniors were smokers—just about the same as the percentage of teenagers who are obese. But it may be even more important to attack teenage smoking than obesity. Fighting obesity is a lifelong battle. But for smoking, adolescence is Armageddon. Only 1 in 10 smokers starts after the age of 18. After the teenage years, the battle is lost.

That's the bad news. The good news is that unlike with obesity, we know what to do.

We didn't always know. In 1997, when 36.5 percent of high school seniors were smokers, a headline in *The Washington Post* said: "Officials Seek a Path to Cut Into Haze of Youth Smoking—The Bottom Line: No One Knows What Works."

Up to that point, efforts to keep teenagers away from cigarettes had focused on health. Public health officials firmly believed that once people knew about how bad smoking was for you, they wouldn't start.

Since 1997, we've learned a lot about how to prevent teenage smoking. The best strategy? Make smoking uncool.

But while health messages have proven good at getting adults to quit, they are not effective at keeping teenagers from starting.

Danger Is Part of Cigarette's Appeal

Any teenager could explain why. For them, a cigarette is not a delivery system for nicotine. It's a delivery system for rebellion. Kids take up smoking to be cool, to impress their friends with their recklessness and defiance of adults. Teenagers don't care about lung cancer—they're immortal. They know that smoking is dangerous. In fact, they overestimate the chances of getting lung cancer. Danger is part of a cigarette's appeal.

Since 1997, we've learned a lot about how to prevent teenage smoking. The best strategy? Make smoking uncool.

One new initiative likely to have a positive effect on both teenage and adult smoking rates will take place this year when Australia will become the first country to regulate that last bastion of cigarette advertising: the pack. All cigarette packs will look alike—a generic olive-green, with big health warnings and the brand name written in small, standardized lettering. For teenagers, who are intensely brand-conscious, plain packs will certainly take some of the allure out of smoking.

Based on the reaction from the tobacco industry, this will hurt. It is waging total war in the World Trade Organization and has mounted legal challenges and information blitzes. . . . Assuming the law survives these challenges, it is likely to spread. New Zealand and Britain are also moving forward with plain packaging legislation. Indian officials have said they will introduce proposals as well.

A Truth Issue

Big Tobacco is desperate because it is well aware of what worked before. The biggest drop in teenage smoking in United States history took place in Florida between 1998 and 2000, as a result of a revolutionary advertising campaign called Truth. Florida had been one of the first states to sue the tobacco companies, and won a settlement that provided the first sustained stream of money to combat teenage smoking. Then 46 states joined together to sue. As part of the larger settlement, the cigarette manufacturers had to release internal documents. These showed that tobacco companies were targeting teenagers—despite denying doing just that.

California had just found success with a campaign that for the first time, portrayed the tobacco companies as the villains. Now Florida would turn that to use for teenagers.

Instead of hiring an ad agency experienced with public health, Florida hired one that specialized in selling stuff, often to teenagers: Crispin Porter + Bogusky. Then it convened a teen tobacco summit. There 600 kids critiqued other states' anti-smoking ads. "The 'smoking will kill you,' 'smoking will turn your teeth yellow' didn't work," said Jared Perez, a tenth-grader at the time from the Tampa Bay area, whom I interviewed in 2009 for my book "Join the Club: How Peer Pressure Can Transform the World." "My reaction, which was typical, was that these were messages you've heard before."

Not so the tobacco industry documents. "These documents were something I'd *never* heard before," Perez said. "It was more compelling than 'smoking is bad for you.' It was a truth issue."

Crispin Porter's ad campaign took the teenage desire for rebellion and turned it against the tobacco companies. The Truth brand would now compete with Marlboro and Camel. For one TV spot, Florida teenagers taped a road trip: they drove to Philip Morris headquarters in Richmond, Va., and asked the security guard at the compound gate if they could talk to the Marlboro Man. Sorry, he's dead, the guard replied. (The model who played the Marlboro man had indeed just died—of lung cancer.) This all went on tape and on the air.

When Florida started the Truth campaign, 27.4 percent of its high school students were smokers. Just two years later, that figure had fallen to 22.6 percent.

Other ads showed kids making prank phone calls to the tobacco-industrial complex. A group of girls called Lucky Strike's advertising account coordinator. "What is the 'lucky' part about Lucky Strike cigarettes?" one girl asks. "Is it because . . . I might live?" After the executive hangs up, the girls laugh maliciously.

Florida's health department then organized SWAT—Students Working Against Tobacco—groups in every county.

"We never said 'don't smoke,'" said Perez, who was later hired to run SWAT. "We got a bunch of kids together to make a statement to the tobacco industry—to rebel against them."

The TV ads and the student groups amplified each other. The television spots made it look like teen rebellion against cigarette companies was sweeping the state. The SWAT groups made it look like the TV ads came from kids, not adults— which boosted their credibility.

When Florida started the Truth campaign, 27.4 percent of its high school students were smokers. Just two years later, that figure had fallen to 22.6 percent; the epidemiologist who evaluated the program called it "perhaps the most effective antitobacco program in the world." Smoking rates have continued to fall, although more slowly. Last year, 14.1 percent of Florida's high school students smoked—about half the pre-Truth number.

Teenagers see plain packs as less attractive, and believe their cigarettes don't taste as good.

With money from the tobacco lawsuit settlement, the truth strategy went national. And it worked nationwide—teen smoking is now half what it was in 1997. But the decline has slowed as states have spent less and less; the vast majority of states have raided their tobacco settlement treasuries and put the money to other use. Even some states that are still spending money have forgotten what works—no doubt at the urging of Big Tobacco—and gone back to health themes. Even Florida has abandoned Truth. Its current ad campaigns feature moving portraits of a young man who died at 30 from smoking, and a girl who lost her father.

Other Ways to Make Smoking Less Cool

The evidence of the Truth campaign's effectiveness is now joined by evidence about two other ways to make smoking less cool.

One is to keep cigarettes out of movies. There's a reason for the sordid history of payments by tobacco manufacturers to moviemakers for product placement (which some researchers argue still goes on). When movie characters smoke, so do teenagers—among kids with nonsmoking parents, the study found that more than half of all smoking initiation comes from exposure to smoking in movies. Leonardo DiCaprio's smoking in "The Titanic" movie will kill far more people than the 1500 who died in the ship accident. The latest study showing the impact also finds that most smoking exposure in movies comes in films rated PG-13. It concludes that if all movies with cigarette smoking were rated R—which means that no filmmaker seeking a youth audience would show it—teen smoking could drop by a whopping 18 percent.

The other idea is generic cigarette packaging. We can't be sure that plain packaging reduces teen smoking, as Australia will be the first to try it. But there's very strong evidence that it will help.

Teenagers love brands, and far more than adults, choose heavily advertised brands to smoke. In countries where cigarette advertising is heavily regulated, the job of brand promotion falls largely to the pack. It's the channel for telling teenagers that American Spirits mark you as hip, or Camel Reds are a he-man smoke, or Virginia Slims or Capri will make you thin and glamorous. (Why do you think so many cigarettes targeting women are called "slims"?)

Plain packs make the name far less prominent, and eliminate the package design that carries all these associations. Teenagers see plain packs as less attractive, and believe their cigarettes don't taste as good. Teenagers label smokers of plain-pack cigarettes as less stylish and social. Girls said that plain-pack cigarettes were less likely to help them stay thin.

Plain packaging also reduces a cigarette's value as a social cue with peers. Every time a teenage girl takes a pack out of her purse to get a cigarette, she is flashing all those brand associations at her friends as well. In short, plain packaging erases the cool factor that comes from smoking a specific brand.

A switch to plain packaging requires no outlay from the government. Nor would re-rating movies in which people smoke. Reviving the Truth campaign is another story—while the student groups such as SWAT are relatively cheap to maintain, TV ads are always costly. But if money for teenage smoking prevention is needed, it's always available from raising cigarette taxes. As a deterrent to teenage smoking, that works, too.

12

Parents Can Influence Teens Not to Smoke

Adi Jaffe

Adi Jaffe is an addiction researcher at the University of California, Los Angeles.

Open and transparent communication between parents and teenagers can influence a youth's decisions not to smoke. A recent study demonstrates that such interaction and communication—if, for instance, a smoking mother acknowledges its struggles to her child—can reduce the chance of persistent smoking. Nonetheless, researchers found that other parents—such as former smoking fathers and nonsmoking mothers—who had preached to their children about its negative consequences were not productive and increased the likelihood of smoking. Parental passivity on the issue, furthermore, can be interpreted by children as approval of smoking. In conclusion, teens are receptive to openness and suspicious of hypocritical preaching when discussing tobacco with their parents.

A recent study assessed the impact parents have over the decisions their teenagers make concerning whether or not to 'experiment' with smoking cigarettes and to continue smoking in the long term, once they have tried it.

Experimenting with smoking represents a form of risk-taking for some teens while it can serve as the onset of long-term chronic cigarette smoking for others. Deciding which group a given teenager is a part of during the initial stage of experimentation is difficult, and figuring out whether it is possible to influence the trajectory of future behavior in teens is the focus of this line of research. The researchers theorized that variations in communication between parents and their teenagers might shine some light on these all-important issues.

So the researchers developed the Family Talk about Smoking paradigm, or FTAS, a method of standardizing the interaction and communication between teen smokers and their parents who had either smoked in the past or currently smoke. It's a neat method that allowed them to study parent-teen interactions in a natural setting.

The FTAS and Assessing Parent-Teen Communication

The FTAS is a 10-minute, semi-structured family interaction paradigm. It employs using a flip card the parent or teen are asked to read to one another. They take turns and each flip card initiates a conversation 'trigger' designed to stimulate smoking-related conversation. The cards focused on five triggers: a) "How people in our family feel about cigarette smoking," (this is read by the teen), "My experiences with cigarette smoking," (by the parent), "How today's teens make decisions about cigarette smoking," (by the teen with this wording used to break open discussion without forcing teen to expose his own experience unless he wants to), and "What parents do if they find out their teen has become a smoker" (by the parent).

The families were given 10 minutes for each topic and were encouraged to use the entire time. Some families used the full ten minutes for some topics, and used less for others while other families sped through them all without lingering on specifics.

It may seem a little contrived and forced, but steps were taken to allow free-flowing conversations between parents and their teens. The FTAS discussion took place in the home environment in order to make the family more comfortable and there was a warm-up exercise to get everyone talking about their family life. When the time came for the FTAS discussion, the field staff left the room and observed the interaction remotely.

So, let's look at what was measured.

A coding system was used to measure the:

- Level of disapproval the teenager received from the parent

- Just how clearly the parent elaborated on consequences for smoking cigarettes

- Whether the parent conveyed to the teen that he expected she would or wouldn't be a smoker

- The quality of personal disclosure by the parent about his own smoking struggles or non-smoking

The teens and their parents were assessed initially and were then revisited 6 months after the baseline assessment to determine whether the family's communication affected teen smoking 6 months later. It's important to note: 90% of parents involved in the study had had some involvement with smoking at some point in their lives.

The researchers found that non-smoking parents who had frequent and quality communication with their teenager about smoking had a consistently positive effect on reducing the chances that their teen will continue to smoke.

The patterns of communication between the teens involved in the study and their parent(s) varied depending on whether the teen (and his parent) were smokers themselves. The teen's receptivity to his parent's attitude and communication about teenage smoking, and about his/her particular smoking, was directly affected by whether the parent smoked currently, or in the past, and what the parent's attitude about it was as well as how openly the parent opened up to his teen about it.

While the study was a controlled assessment of teen-parent communication about smoking cigarettes, it's important to note its implications for family communication about substance abuse, and other taboo issues. There's no doubt that communication is extremely important when it comes to these topics and that open communication often leads to better outcomes than ignoring or avoiding these issues.

The Results: Talking to Teens About Smoking Can Help if It's Done Right

Communication patterns and their effect depended greatly on who the teen was speaking to—with mothers, expressing more positive expectancies about cigarette smoking predicted more persistent smoking while with fathers more disapproval during conversations predicted lower chances of persistent smoking.

The researchers found that non-smoking parents who had frequent and quality communication with their teenager about smoking had a consistently positive effect on reducing the chances that their teen will continue to smoke. However, the results revealed that if the parent smoked their influence through communication was much more complicated. For fathers, past smoking combined with a lot of teen disclosure predicted much greater likelihood of continued smoking—it's the "war story" sort of effect with parent and teen sharing experiences and little disapproval leading to no reduction in experimentation. For currently smoking mothers the important factor was also disclosure but this time by the parent—if the mother shared little about her experiences, the effect on teen smoking was small but if she shared a lot, the odds of persistent teen smoking went way down. When non-smoking mothers talked a lot about the consequences of smoking, the probability of persistent teen smoking went up—kids don't like being preached to.

This research seems to carry the following message— don't preach if you haven't been there and don't be hypocritical if you have.

What does it all mean?

Overall, the study's results suggest that teens are highly suspect of hypocritical preaching and are very much influenced by communication patterns with their parents. Specifically, the study revealed that when a mother was a current smoker, if she communicated openly to her teenager that she had struggles about smoking and the difficulty of quitting, there was a positive effect on the teen's eventual decision to stop. But for former smoking fathers and non-smoking mothers, talking at length about the teen's experiences smoking and about the negative consequences of smoking respectively were not productive and actually increased the probability that the teen would still be smoking six months later.

> As the authors note: ". . . current smoking mothers who are highly disclosing may acknowledge their own struggles around smoking and their difficulty asking their teens to 'do what I say not what I do.' Openness about this struggle may help adolescents deal with the issue of 'mixed messages' when a parent is a smoker. In contrast, the impact of maternal elaboration of rules may be attenuated when mothers have been active smokers because the parents' own behavior is contradictory." Reducing hypocritical messages and communicating openly about these difficult issues seems to be the way to go.

When taking all these findings into account it would seem that passivity on the part of a parent rather than communicating with the teen seems to be received by the teen as a silent approval of smoking. However a parent's open and transparent sharing with his teen about his own regretted decisions, and the difficulty that has resulted, can have a very positive effect on the decisions the teen makes.

The Bigger Picture

If these things are true with cigarette smoking, would they not also be true regarding experimentation with other substances? Can parents open up about their experiences to their teens, expose their difficulties and vulnerabilities, and give the teen the gift of a loving parent's experience?

Maybe more importantly, when thinking about the right ways to engage in teen-parent communication about difficult issues, a little insight into family dynamics that may have an impact on the discussion seems crucial. I often get questions from parents I know about the most appropriate way to talk to kids about drug use. This research seems to carry the following message—don't preach if you haven't been there and don't be hypocritical if you have—open communication that guides the teen toward the desired behavior without letting them discount the impact of their choices seems the best idea.

Before we go, it's important to note that this study used only a six-month follow-up and that future studies should really examine more long-term effects of family communication patterns in order to increase our confidence in these results. It's possible that family communication can have a long-lasting effect or that it needs to be re-enforced on an ongoing basis. This study doesn't tell us much about that.

13

Penalizing Minors for Cigarette Use May Be Counterproductive

Jessica Guilfoyle

Jessica Guilfoyle is a research associate at the Campaign for Tobacco-Free Kids in Washington, DC.

Youth-penalty laws for minors that are caught purchasing, using, or possessing tobacco products are problematic. Supported by the tobacco industry, many of these laws replace more effective measures to reduce youth smoking and hinder the enforcement of other forms of tobacco control. Additionally, penalizing children who become hooked due to the aggressive marketing tactics of the tobacco companies is unfair and stigmatizing, shifting the blame away from businesses that profit from these actions. Overall, existing and future youth-penalty laws must be thoroughly evaluated to ensure that they do not undermine tobacco control or laws aiming to protect kids and punish those who sell tobacco to minors.

All the states prohibit retailers from selling tobacco products to minors. In addition, 46 states have also enacted laws that subject kids who purchase, use, or possess cigarettes or other tobacco products with various penalties ranging from small fines to jail time. Massachusetts, Nevada, New Jersey, and New York have not implemented any such youth penalty laws.

Some of these laws were proposed to help reduce underage smoking and other tobacco use by making kids more directly and personally responsible for buying or using tobacco products. In many cases, however, the tobacco companies and their allies have supported these youth-penalty laws as alternatives to other laws that would produce larger and more rapid reductions in underage tobacco use. Even worse, the tobacco companies have used the passage of youth-penalty laws to get additional provisions enacted that make implementing or enforcing other tobacco control efforts more difficult. Accordingly, both existing youth-penalty laws and any new proposals must be carefully evaluated to make sure they will not end up impeding other tobacco control efforts or otherwise diverting attention from the need for strong laws aimed at protecting children and punishing adults who sell to children.

In addition, youth-penalty laws can unfairly punish or stigmatize children who became addicted either when they were too young to know better or as a direct result of the tobacco industry's aggressive marketing to kids. In that way, youth-penalty laws shift blame from industry promotional activities to the victims. Similarly, youth penalty laws treat children as the primary wrongdoers, instead of focusing on those adults and businesses who profit from knowingly selling tobacco products to kids.

Virtually all of the new youth-penalty laws fail to ensure that teens already addicted to cigarettes or other tobacco products have somewhere they can go to get help quitting so they can obey the law.

Concerns with Youth-Penalty Laws

Many of the existing laws and new proposals to establish youth penalties have major problems:

- Because of tobacco company influence, youth-penalty laws often end up being passed instead of much more effective tobacco control strategies, such as increasing the price of cigarettes, restricting tobacco company marketing, or implementing new programs and counter-advertising to prevent and reduce tobacco use among kids.

- Establishing new youth penalties can divert the police from their efforts to stop retailers from illegally selling tobacco products to kids, especially since the new laws typically fail to provide any additional enforcement resources. It also appears that youth-penalty laws are more difficult to enforce systematically than sanctions against retailers; and they can create confusion as to who should be responsible for enforcing which laws relating to tobacco product sales to youth. On the other hand, stopping retailers who profit from selling to underage buyers is a proven way to reduce both youth access to tobacco and underage use, and such sales can be stopped only by ongoing rigorous enforcement.

- Laws that penalize children for possession of tobacco products that call for excessive penalties or are not strictly enforced can breed disrespect for the law by young people, thereby having a negative effect.

- In at least twelve states, the youth-penalty laws directly preempt more effective state and local tobacco control laws already in effect and forbid cities and towns from passing any new tobacco control laws that are broader or stronger than the state's.

- Youth-penalty laws sometimes make it extremely difficult to enforce the laws forbidding tobacco sales to kids because they make it illegal to use underage buyers in "sting" operations to identify retailers that knowingly sell to kids (which is the most effective way to catch these lawbreaking retailers). Some of the laws even make it illegal for anyone but the police or other specified state enforcement personnel to run operations to identify retailers that illegally sell to kids, thereby blocking community groups, researchers, or state health officers from monitoring retailer compliance.

- Some of the new youth-penalty laws actually subject underage smokers to hundreds of dollars in fines, court hearings, and even jail time (e.g. in Oklahoma and Idaho). Such excessive penalties and prosecutions against children are even more unreasonable when little is done to restrict the tobacco companies' aggressive marketing efforts that reach and influence children or to stop retailers who illegally sell tobacco products to children.

- Virtually all of the new youth-penalty laws fail to ensure that teens already addicted to cigarettes or other tobacco products have somewhere they can go to get help quitting so they can obey the law. In fact, most of the laws do not even give addicted underage users who violate the law the option or opportunity of entering a formal cessation program. This focus on punishing underage addicts rather than helping them get the treatment and assistance they need to quit is not only mean-spirited but medically foolish.

- The move to penalize children has taken place without any clear empirical evidence that these laws actually reduce tobacco use among children. The impact of the laws now in effect should be carefully studied before additional ones are enacted.

Evidence Addressing Penalizing Youth for Tobacco Possession, Use, and Purchase of Tobacco

- A study done in Texas in 2006 examined the perspectives of Texas youth after having been cited for tobacco possession. Although youth cited acknowledged that the law was meant to deter youth from smoking, they also indicated that there was no purpose to it and that it could actually lead to continuation. The study further suggests that youth cited for possession are not deterred because they are addicted to cigarettes, implying that interventions should focus more on cessation programs.

- After examining New Jersey youth penalty laws, a 2004 study suggested that cessation treatment rather than punishment may be a more effective measure to reduce youth smoking. It further suggests that youth may be deterred from seeking help for their addiction should they be punished for breaking the law.

- A 2003 study reviewing literature and reasons for youth penalty laws concluded that such laws were unlikely to "significantly reduce youth smoking." The reasons given included a low likelihood of being caught, uncertain punishment, delay between detection and punishment, and high chances of youth being able to evade detection.

- A *Journal of Drug Education* study reviewed the debate regarding youth penalty laws. While it acknowledges that such laws can be effective in conjunction with programs that reduce youth access, it also suggests that more research needs to be done studying the effects of the youth penalties on kids.

Organizations to Contact

The editors have compiled the following list of organizations concerned with the issues debated in this book. The descriptions are derived from materials provided by the organizations. All have publications or information available for interested readers. The list was compiled on the date of publication of the present volume; names, addresses, phone and fax numbers, and e-mail and Internet addresses may change. Be aware that many organizations take several weeks or longer to respond to inquiries, so allow as much time as possible.

American Cancer Society (ACS)
250 Williams St. NW, Atlanta, GA   30303
(800) 227-2345
website: www.cancer.org

The American Cancer Society (ACS) is the nationwide community-based voluntary health organization dedicated to eliminating cancer as a major health problem by preventing the disease, saving lives, and diminishing suffering from cancer, through research, education, advocacy, and service. A number of publications concerned with smoking, including teen smoking, are available through the Society and on its website, including reports, surveys, and position papers.

American Legacy Foundation
1724 Massachusetts Ave. NW, Washington, DC   20036
website: www.legacyforhealth.org

Created in 1999 out of the landmark Master Settlement Agreement (MSA) between the tobacco industry, forty-six state governments, and five US territories, the American Legacy Foundation works to encourage youth to reject tobacco use as a part of their lives and to assist and empower smokers of all ages to quit. Their programs include Truth, a youth smoking prevention campaign, and EX, a health program that seeks to

communicate with current smokers in a nonthreatening manner, encouraging them to approach quitting in ways not considered in the past. The Foundation maintains a library of scientific reports, surveys, fact sheets, and publications related to
tobacco use, its dangers, and cessation.

American Lung Association
1301 Pennsylvania Ave. NW, Suite 800
Washington, DC   20004
(202) 785-3355 • fax: (202) 452-1805
website: www.lung.org

The mission of the American Lung Association is to prevent
lung disease and promote lung health. Founded in 1904 to
fight tuberculosis, the organization today fights lung disease in
all its forms, with special emphasis on asthma, tobacco control, and environmental health. Reports, studies, position papers, and materials focused on smoking cessation are available
on its website.

Americans for Nonsmokers' Rights (ANR)
2530 San Pablo Ave., Suite J, Berkeley, CA   94702
(510) 841-3032 • fax: (510) 841-3071
website: www.no-smoke.org

Americans for Nonsmokers' Rights (ANR) is a national lobbying organization dedicated to securing the rights of nonsmokers, taking on the tobacco industry at all levels of government,
protecting nonsmokers from exposure to secondhand smoke,
and preventing tobacco addiction among youth. ANR pursues
an action-oriented program of policy and legislation. It pub-
lishes a quarterly newsletter, *UPDATE!*, and provides information on a variety of smoke-free issues on its website.

Campaign for Tobacco-Free Kids
1400 I St. NW, Washington, DC   20005
(202) 296-5469
website: www.tobaccofreekids.org

The Campaign for Tobacco-Free Kids seeks to reduce tobacco use and its devastating consequences in the United States and around the world. By changing public attitudes and public policies on tobacco, they hope to prevent youth from smoking, help smokers quit, and protect everyone from secondhand smoke. Publications include press releases, fact sheets, and reports, many of which are available on the organization's website.

Cato Institute
1000 Massachusetts Ave. NW, Washington, DC   20001-5403
(202) 842-0200
website: www.cato.org

The Cato Institute is a libertarian public policy research foundation dedicated to limiting the control of government and protecting individual liberty. Its quarterly magazine, *Regulation*, has published articles and letters questioning the accuracy of US Environmental Protection Agency studies on the dangers of secondhand smoke. The *Cato Journal* is published by the Institute three times a year, and policy analysis papers are published periodically. Online resources and articles are updated continually.

**FORCES International (Fight Ordinances and
Restrictions to Control and Eliminate Smoking)**
PO Box 4267, Kaneohe, HI   96744
(808) 721-8384
website: www.forces.org

FORCES International fights against smoking ordinances and restrictions designed to eventually eliminate smoking, and it works to increase public awareness of smoking-related legislation. It opposes any state or local ordinance it feels is not fair to those who choose to smoke. Although FORCES does not advocate smoking, it asserts that an individual has the right to choose to smoke and that smokers should be accommodated where and when possible. The FORCES website maintains an extensive online library of articles, books, and reviews, as well as recommended publications on a variety of subjects, including smokers' rights issues.

Heartland Institute

One South Wacker Dr. #2740, Chicago, IL 60606
(312) 377-4000 • fax: (312) 377-5000
e-mail: think@heartland.org
website: http://heartland.org

Founded in 1984, the Heartland Institute is a nonprofit research and education organization with the mission to discover, develop, and promote free-market solutions to social and economic problems. The Institute advocates for smokers' rights, charging antismoking groups with using propaganda and exaggerations to promote tobacco control. On its website, its Smoking Lounge provides information for tobacco users, covering issues such as smoking bans, taxes, and secondhand smoke. The Heartland Institute also published a book defending smokers, *Please Don't Poop in My Salad.*

impacTEEN

University of Illinois at Chicago
Institute for Health Research and Policy
1747 West Roosevelt Rd., Room 558, M/C 275
Chicago, IL 60608
(312) 413-0475 • fax: (312) 355-2801
e-mail: impcteen@uic.edu
website: www.impacteen.org

impacTeen is an interdisciplinary partnership of health experts with specialties in such areas as economics, etiology, epidemiology, law, political science, public policy, psychology, and sociology. The project, part of the Robert Wood Johnson Foundation's Bridging the Gap: Research Informing Practice and Policy for Healthy Youth Behavior, focuses on economic, environmental, and policy influences on youth substance use, obesity, and physical activity. Materials available through impacTEEN include research papers, presentations, policy briefs, reports, and other data related to smoking and youth.

National Institute on Drug Abuse (NIDA)

Office of Science Policy and Communications
Public Information and Liaison Branch
6001 Executive Blvd., Room 5213, MSC 9561
Bethesda, MD   20892 9561
(301) 443-1124
website: www.drugabuse.gov

The National Institute on Drug Abuse (NIDA), a federal scientific research institute, is the largest supporter of the world's research on drug abuse and addiction. The Institute addresses fundamental and essential questions about drug abuse, including tracking emerging drug-use trends, understanding how drugs work in the brain and body, developing and testing new drug treatments and prevention approaches, and disseminating findings to the general public and special populations. NIDA maintains a library of materials regarding smoking and other addictive substances geared toward youth, parents, educators, doctors, and other health professionals, as well as researchers.

US Food and Drug Administration (FDA)

10903 New Hampshire Ave., Silver Spring, MD   20993
(888) 463-6332
website: www.fda.gov

The US Food and Drug Administration (FDA) is one of the nation's oldest consumer protection agencies. Its mission is to promote and protect the public health by ensuring that products introduced to the market are safe and effective; monitoring products for continued safety after they are in use; and helping the public get the accurate, science-based information needed to improve health. On the FDA's website, its section on tobacco products offers information on marketing and labeling of tobacco, electronic cigarettes, youth smoking, and other issues.

Bibliography

Books

Joseph L. Bast *Please Don't Poop in My Salad.* Chicago: Heartland Institute, 2006.

Allan M. Brandt *The Cigarette Century: The Rise, Fall, and Deadly Persistence of the Product That Defined America.* New York: Basic Books, 2007.

Eric Burns *The Smoke of the Gods: A Social History of Tobacco.* Philadelphia: Temple University Press, 2007.

Martha A. Derthick *Up in Smoke: From Legislation to Litigation in Tobacco Politics,* 3rd ed. Washington, DC: CQ Press, 2012.

Sharon Y. Eubanks and Stanton A. Glantz *Bad Acts: The Racketeering Case Against the Tobacco Industry.* Washington, DC: American Public Health Association, 2012.

Chris Harrald and Fletcher Watkins *The Cigarette Book: The History and Culture of Smoking.* New York: Skyhorse Publishing, 2010.

Judith Longstaff Mackay, Michael Eriksen, and Hanna Ross *The Tobacco Atlas,* 4th ed. Atlanta: American Cancer Society, 2012.

Robert N. Proctor *Golden Holocaust: Origins of the Cigarette Catastrophe and the Case for Abolition.* Berkeley: University of California Press, 2011.

Vanessa Rogers

A Little Book of Tobacco: Activities to Explore Smoking Issues with Young People. Philadelphia: Jessica Kingsley Publishers, 2012.

Michael Schwalbe

Smoke Damage: Voices from the Front Lines of America's Tobacco Wars. Madison, WI: Borderland Books, 2011.

Clete Snell

Peddling Poison: The Tobacco Industry and Kids. Westport, CN: Praeger, 2005.

Christopher Snowdon

Velvet Glove, Iron Fist: A History of Anti-Smoking. Ripon, UK: Little Dice, 2009.

Periodicals and Internet Sources

Steve Chapman

"Sweet Lies About Kids and Smoking," *Reason*, September 28, 2009.

Matthew Creamer

"Anti-Smoking Campaigns Work, So Don't Quit Now," *Advertising Age*, January 16, 2012.

Brent Green

"The Future of Nicotine Addiction: When Smokers Become Vapers," *Huffington Post*, April 1, 2013. www.huffingtonpost.com.

John Hillard

"Despite Health Risks, New Policy Tolerates Student Smoking Outside Brookline High," *Wicked Local Brookline*, September 30, 2010. www.wickedlocal.com/brookline.

 Smoking*

Steve Kaniger — "To Reach the Young, Anti-Smoking Ads Fight Vice with Vice," *Las Vegas Sun*, July 13, 2010.

Roxanne Khamsi — "Smoking Is a Drag at the Box Office," *Scientific American*, October 10, 2011.

Abbey Lewis — "Cracking the Flavor Code," *CSP Magazine*, December 2009.

Chris McNamara — "Teen Anti-Smoking Campaign Keeps Its Cool," *Chicago Tribune*, July 28, 2010.

Patti Neighmond — "One Teen's Struggle to Quit," National Public Radio, November 6, 2008. www.npr.org.

Julie Carr Smyth — "Colleges May Ban Smoking," *Salon*, June 28, 2012. www.salon.com.

Jennifer Van Pelt — "Graphic Antismoking Images: Will They Work?" *Social Work Today*, July 2012.

Duff Wilson — "Teenage Smoking Rates Spur Calls to Renew Anti-Tobacco Campaigns," *New York Times*, July 8, 2010. http://prescriptions.blogs.nytimes.com.

Index